The
Grandmother
Principles

The
Grandmother
Principles

Suzette Haden Elgin

Abbeville Press   Publishers   New York   London   Paris

....

FOR MY GRANDCHILDREN:
ROSAMOND, JOSEPHA, GIDEON, WILLIAM, JUSTIN,
CAITLIN, KARI, CORY, CASEY, AND KATHRYN

....

Editor: Jacqueline Decter
Designer: Celia Fuller
Production Editor: Meredith Wolf Schizer
Production Director: Hope Koturo

First edition
2 4 6 8 10 9 7 5 3

Needlepoint on cover by Celia Fuller.
Cover photograph by Gamma One.
For cartoon credits, see page 220.

Library of Congress Cataloging-in-Publication Data
Elgin, Suzette Haden.
The grandmother principles / Suzette Haden Elgin.
p.   cm.
Includes bibliographical references and index.
ISBN 0-7892-0431-2
1. Grandmothers. 2. Grandparenting. I. Title.
HQ759.9.E44   1998
306.874'5—dc21   98-8072

Contents

◨

PREFACE

6

INTRODUCTION

9

Chapter 1

Thinking Like a Grandmother

25

Chapter 2

Nudging, Nagging, and
Nattering—Do You Have To?

50

Chapter 3

Emotional Work

66

Chapter 4

Resources—Money, Time,
and Energy

92

Chapter 5

Emergency Procedures

122

Chapter 6

In Sickness and in Health

137

Chapter 7

Mythmaking and
Story Telling

158

Chapter 8

Recording Your Family
History and Passing It On

173

CONCLUSION

188

APPENDIX

Teaching the Grannycrafts

195

REFERENCES AND
SUGGESTED READING

207

INDEX

211

Preface

When Sheila Kitzinger wrote *Becoming A Grandmother*, she didn't just do it off the top of her head. She thoroughly investigated the grandmother role all over this wide world, with the help of many real grandmothers, and she discovered:

IN MOST TRADITIONAL CULTURES, GRANDMOTHERS ARE PEOPLE OF IMMENSE IMPORTANCE AND AUTHORITY.

That has a lovely ring to it, don't you think? At the moment, however, grandmothers in the "Western" world can only look at that sentence, sigh, and say, "They are? Well, good for *them!*"

Not that there are no grandmothers in our cultures who are people of immense importance and authority. Of course there are. But it's an individual matter, and one that depends on each individual woman. It's not something automatic. It's not something women can look forward to and take for granted. It's not a mantle of status that will be wrapped around them just because they *are* grandmothers. We have no "grandmotherhood" ceremony to mark the occasion and announce it as something to celebrate. In fact, in our youth-obsessed society the whole question of what a grandmother is and does has become so problematic that many women, hearing that they're about to become one, don't know whether to rejoice or run for cover!

I think they should rejoice; no question about it. This book is intended to clarify the grandmother muddle a bit, and to champion three basic propositions:

❖ First, that grandmothers in the United States and other modern, "nontraditional" cultures *should* be looked upon as "people of immense importance and authority."
❖ Second, that becoming a grandmother is an occasion for celebration.
❖ And third, that *being* a grandmother, though it brings responsibilities and the occasional rough patch, though it's a role that has to be learned and takes some getting used to, can and should be a delight.

Credit for this book does not belong to me alone; I had a lot of help. Special thanks go to my agent, Jeff McCartney, and to my editor, Jackie Decter, for all their patience and guidance as the book was being written. Thanks are due to my husband, my children, and my grandchildren (all ten of them), who provided me with the experience I needed to write this book and were helpful and supportive while I got it done.

Above all, I owe a debt of gratitude to my own grandmother Bertha Letha Motley Lewis, who started me down this road with a sure hand, a magnificent example, and an unconditional love.

Suzette Haden Elgin
P.O. Box 1137
Huntsville, Arkansas 72740-1137
ocls@ipa.net

"*Gosh, Grandma, what a big office you have!*"

Introduction

🍂 Why We Need This Book

🍂 The Grandmothering Problem

When I was a little girl (I was born in 1936), everybody knew exactly how to spot a grandmother. Grandmothers were Old Ladies, period. They had gray or white hair, they had wrinkles, and they wore dresses, usually dresses that buttoned down the front. My own grandmother got up every day at 4:30 A.M. and put on a dress and hose and high heels. Even when she was working in the garden; even when she went fishing at the river. Rich or poor, fat or slender, grandmothers in those days were Old Ladies, and they dressed and behaved accordingly.

Grandmothers in the 1930s and 1940s either knew how to do everything or were very good at pretending that they did. Their families doted on them or were terrified of them, often both. We expected grandmothers to be neat and clean and sweet smelling at all times. We expected them to be experts in all the homemaking arts and crafts and sciences, and the idea that they might get into any kind of trouble never crossed our minds. After all, they were *elderly;* they were long past the trouble stage.

This goes a long way toward explaining why a woman's first thought today when she learns that she's going to be a grandmother is often "But I'm not that *old!*" Gail Sheehy, in an article called "Congratulations, You're a Grandmother!" says it's the shock of being "pushed to the front of the generational train." She's quite right; for many women, it does feel like being pushed. One minute they're young or middle-aged, and the next—all of a sudden, without any preparation or transition—here comes a label that they've always associated only with old age.

Thanks to television and movies, that prototype grandmother concept is still with us, after a vague fashion. I look quite a bit like the grandmothers of my childhood. Not long ago, as I was leaving a Wal-Mart store, I said a polite hello to a group of teenage boys on their way in. And as the door closed behind me I heard one of them say to the others, "Now *that* is what a grandmother is supposed to look like!" It warmed my heart to hear it, but he wasn't quite right; close, but not quite. Because, despite my white hair and my wrinkles, I was wearing slacks. The grandmothers of my childhood would have cut their throats before going out in public in slacks; most lived their entire lives without ever putting on a single pair.

Grandmothers today are often a different matter entirely. Today, when mothers may be no more than sixteen or seventeen years old, we see many grandmothers who are still in their thirties or forties. Not only do we see grandmothers in pants, we see them in shorts, and in bikinis. White hair and wrinkles are far in their future. They look more like somebody's sister than somebody's grandparent. It's not as easy for them to inspire awe as it was for the classic grandmothers of the past.

And no longer does a typical household have at least one very old lady in residence or living close by, finishing out her life and serving as an information resource and role model for the younger women coming along after her. Today's very old ladies tend to be of two kinds: those who are in nursing homes and retirement centers and "snowbird" parks (often halfway across the continent from their families), and those who are seizing the opportunity to do all the things they always longed to do—like climbing mountains and trekking through rain forests—and are even less conveniently located. Even when elderly ladies stay put themselves, families today move so often that they're not likely to be right at hand. It's no longer easy for women to learn how to *act* like grandmothers.

The competent grandmother shortage is even worse for the multitude of single mothers. Whatever their reasons for parenting without a father on deck, they have only half as many chances to be blessed with access to a grandmother as mothers with partners do.

Suppose you happen to be one of these junior grandmothers, without a wrinkle to your name. What are you to do? How are you to proceed? Suppose (whatever your actual age) you are a woman whose mothering came for the most part from a television set. Many women meet that description today, through no fault of their own, because their mothers were always desperately busy and often worked outside the home as well as within it. Suppose you are someone who was forced to leave the care of your own child to a relative or sitter while you worked long hours, perhaps at more than one job; suppose that as a result most of your practice in mothering skills was pretty much restricted to putting teeny-tiny lingerie and evening gowns on your Barbie dolls. How do you manage? Where do you go to get grandmother lessons?

There was a day when a woman without an experienced older lady to turn to for help could buy or borrow fat books that would serve pretty well as stand-ins for a live grandmother, at least well enough to get her started. Today those "housekeeping compendiums," even when they can be found, have ceased to be a very useful resource. Most of us no longer need to know how to churn butter or get milk stains out of linen-and-lace baby dresses.

The books and magazines I see that claim to be for today's grandmothers often miss the mark. They tell you how to choose a theme park to take the grandkids to during your annual two-week visit. They tell you how how to pick a suitable stock to start your grandchild's investment portfolio. They tell you how to handle the resentment your grandchild's mother feels because she isn't as beautiful as you are and her figure isn't nearly as good as yours and she can't afford to dress as well as you do. These are useful skills, and they may represent tasks you'll be taking on one of these days. But they're not the basics. They're the frills, way out on the edge of grandmother wit and wisdom and how-to.

Basic grandmother skills are rapidly disappearing, that's the problem, and we can't do without them. If we don't take action to save them now, we're going to be in serious trouble down the road. Since we can't wave a magic wand and produce competent grandmothers-in-residence on demand, we have to turn to other sources of information. What we need—fast—is a modern (and shorter, and less grim) version of those old-fashioned compendiums, based on a set of guidelines that can be applied to every aspect of grandmothering and written for today's woman. What we need is *this* book.

✣ Why I'm Qualified to Write This Book

You don't know me; I've never had the pleasure of meeting you and spending time with you. Let me introduce myself.

✣ My Grandmother Merit Badges

I have ten grandchildren of my own. Four of them are less than an hour away from my home in Arkansas, so that I can be regularly involved in their raising and I am on standby at all times for grandmother duty. Four are in California, and two are in New Zealand, providing me with experience in the skills of long-distance grandmothering that are so crucial for our far-flung modern families.

My California grandchildren lost their father very suddenly and had to learn the lessons of bitter grief and agonizing loss at far too early an age. Until recently they lived only a hundred yards away from me; I was with their mother when the third one was born, and I pre-schooled the first three. Seeing them move away (for excellent reasons) wasn't easy, but I learned from it. Four of my grandchildren, whose father is Laotian and Buddhist, live in a multicultural and multilingual household. The other two—the New Zealand ones—live the perfect and uncomplicated life of the *Dick and Jane* books. I have average grandchildren and gifted ones, tall ones and short ones, talented ones and ones whose talents have yet to appear. I have grandchildren living in upper-middle-class comfort and grandchildren who know what it is to have scrambled eggs for dinner four nights in a row. Some of my grandchildren have been home-schooled (as were some of my children); some are happy in traditional school settings. Most, to my great joy, are healthy in every way, but I have one grandchild who struggles with a chronic illness. I have a more than ample assortment, you see.

And I have had plenty of experience with the problems modern parents face. I raised two sons, two daughters, and at times a stepson through every variety of situations and circumstances, most of them difficult and some almost unbelievable. Any problem I haven't yet seen among my grandchildren is sure to be one I have already had to deal with as I was bringing up their parents.

✤ My Writer Merit Badges

You can trust me to get you safely to the end of this book. I have written and published more than two dozen books—novels, nonfiction books, and textbooks—and I do know how it's done. I took up book writing as a way of getting myself through college while I still had four—sometimes five—youngsters at home to look after. I won't lecture you, and I won't preach at you. I won't ask you to settle for platitudes and vapors. I won't pretend that grandmothering is never anything but moonlight and roses. I will give you real information in abundance, solid and practical and useful, as clearly as I know how. And because I know how busy you are, I'll do it as briefly as possible.

✦ My Own Two Grandmothers

As you know by now, I had one classic grandmother. My maternal grandmother, Bertha Letha Motley Lewis, would have won a Grandmothering Olympics hands-down. I spent the first five years of my life in her constant company and a lot of time with her thereafter, and I remember every single thing she taught me. When she made turkey stuffing (which she called "turkey dressing"), she began by making buttermilk biscuits from scratch, to be crumbled for the stuffing. That meant starting at three-thirty Thanksgiving morning, and she did. For Christmas she made box after box after box of fudge and caramels and stuffed dates, carefully layered between sheets of waxed paper— from scratch. Her church counted on her for Easter lilies, and she provided them. The day she found a rattlesnake by her woodshed, she put her high-heeled shoe on its neck, chopped it in half with her hoe, pitched the corpse in the garbage can, and went on to tend her rosebushes. Neither I nor anyone else, so far as I know, would ever have thought of disobeying her. She was that sort of grandmother, and I adored her.

I also had a grandmother of the other sort. I know from photographs that my Grandmother Diana had the specified white hair and wrinkles, but that's about all I know. She and my grandfather were separated, though never divorced; I lived in Missouri and she lived in California. She was a total stranger to me. She never wrote, she never called, she never sent a Christmas card, she never came to visit. If she invited *us* to visit, no one ever told me. The only gift I ever received from her was a rhinestone necklace that she sent me when I graduated from high school and that I have still. She died without my ever having met her. She either didn't know how to do long-distance grandmothering or didn't choose to. I will never know which, and that's a shame. But she did an excellent job of showing me how *not* to grandmother, and that has turned out to be useful for this book.

There: that's who I am and how I came to know about grandmothering. We can now move on to consider . . .

The Four Basic Grandmothers

Grandmothers follow four basic patterns, whether they live next door or a thousand miles away. Let's take a brief look at all four, so that you can choose the one that you think would fit you best. You'll want to tailor it to your own needs, of course, but the broad outlines below will get you started.

The Traditional Grandmother

Traditional Grandmothers today don't necessarily look old in the way the grandmothers of my childhood did. But they don't dye their hair to hide the gray, they don't worry about wrinkles, and they don't dress like their daughters dress. They are glad to baby-sit their grandchildren—within reason. They always send gifts and/or cards on holidays and

"I like to think that these old recipes you're learning at Granny's knee may someday help you to work off executive stress from your big, big business career."

birthdays. When someone writes to these women, they answer the letter; when someone leaves a message on the answering machine, they return the call. When asked for advice, they give it gladly; when they feel that advice is needed and nobody does ask, they go ahead and offer it anyway—gently. Going out with a Traditional Grandmother is a pleasure, because she will always be courteous and pleasant, and it will always be possible to be proud of her.

*"I made it with my food processor, cordless blender, and microwave.
If you want, I'll e-mail you the recipe."*

✖️ The Ultramodern Grandmother

Ultramodern Grandmothers may be any age from thirty to ninety, but they don't look like stereotypical elderly ladies. When they have white hair, it will be dramatically and fashionably styled. They either have no wrinkles at all (by the luck of the draw or by facelift) or glory in their wrinkles on the grounds that wrinkles show character. They dress in the Very Latest Thing. They do not hesitate to tell their offspring that they prefer *not* to be called Grandmother, if that's how they feel about it, and to specify what they do wish to be called. They will baby-sit if it suits them, but only if there are no restrictions—that is, if they are absolutely in charge while they do it. They rarely write postal letters, although they may send e-mail; they telephone often and will usually send holiday cards. They offer advice without hesitation, whether asked for it or not; they are quite ready to talk about sex and drugs and religion and sports and what's cool. Going out with an Ultramodern Grandmother is an adventure for the grandchildren, because she may take them places their parents would never let them go; they'd be wise not to expect that she'll be "nice" at all times, however.

✖️ The Eccentric Grandmother

All bets are off with this kind of grandmother. She may wear her hair flowing down her back all the way to her waist, she may wear it in braids, she may shave her head. She may dress in anything whatsoever; she may wear cowboy boots. What she does in the way of writing and calling and remembering gift occasions can be anything from punctilious dotting of every I and crossing of every T to inventing occasions of her own and honoring only those or ignoring the entire apparatus of such practices. Sometimes she'll baby-sit, sometimes she won't, according to rules of her own devising. Going out with an Eccentric Grandmother can be wildly exciting or terrifying or both at once, and it can make everyone present want to pretend they're not with her. She may or may not supply advice; when she does, it's a good idea to think carefully

before taking it. She may very well get in trouble, sometimes in ways that no one in the family could have imagined.

❧ The Overburdened Grandmother

This fourth grandmother variety is a woman who never gets around to choosing one of the other three grandmothering styles. She could of course work out some new grandmother flavor of her own instead, but she doesn't do that either. Sometimes the explanation is that she's so young she really needs to be grandmothered herself instead of taking on the role. Sometimes it's because she is just frail; not everyone comes into this world strong and vigorous and filled with energy and joy and gumption, and not all who do arrive that way reach grandmotherhood unscathed. And sometimes it's because she is so busy, or so totally disorganized, that she can scarcely find time to breathe. However she looks and whatever she does, she always seems fretful and worried and rushed and absent-minded; often she seems very tired as well. She may send cards and letters and gifts, and she may call—but she will do it at the last possible minute, and whoever is on the receiving end will feel guilty. Going places with an Overburdened Grandmother or having her baby-sit won't ordinarily be much fun, because everyone involved will feel bad about the trouble they're putting her through and the distress they're causing her.

This can be a good cover for a woman who truly wants nothing to do with grandmothering, since it guarantees that nobody will rely on her to chop wood and haul water on any regular basis. It can also be the unfortunate and genuine situation of a woman who doesn't quite know how to proceed and who really *is* overburdened. If you tend toward this type, and it's genuine rather than a put-on, stay with me; I'll show you how to fix that. By the time you get to the end of this book you'll see clearly that you have other, better choices. If you *are* trying to avoid the whole grandmother role, please stay with me anyway; I'd like a chance to persuade you to change your mind.

🕊️ Why Grandmothering Is a Good Investment

Let's suppose for a minute that you're strongly considering settling for being an Overburdened Grandmother, in the hope that your family will then give up and leave you alone. Or you're considering going away, perhaps to Australia or the outermost reaches of Maine, and leaving *them* alone. Let's suppose that you're thinking, *Why in the world should I bother with the grandmother role?*

Feeling that way doesn't mean that you're a selfish person, in spite of what you may read and what well-meaning friends who love grandmothering (or who do it, grimly, because they consider it their duty) may tell you. It's a sensible and legitimate question. After all, the reason you are a grandmother now is probably that you've already devoted a sizable portion of your life to looking after the concerns and needs of other people, not all of whom were fascinating company, and not all of whom appreciated your efforts. You may very well feel that you've had it up to here with all that and that it's now time for you to do *your* thing.

I can understand that perfectly; there are days when I feel exactly the same way. Every sane grandmother does. However, it's possible to be an active, competent grandmother and do your own thing too. Most of the time that "Let me out of here!" feeling comes from the very problem that this book is designed to remedy: the lack of adequate information about grandmothering. I can demonstrate to you that the joys of being a grandmother far outweigh the burdens—if you know what you're doing. I'm here to show you that successful grandmothering does not have to be hard, so that you can more calmly consider the *benefits* of grandmothering.

❧ The Benefits for Your Children (the Chadults)

Your grandkids' parents—your own children, whether seventeen or forty, and their partners—face many problems that you have already faced. It may be that everything you did when those problems were yours was wrong. That's fine! You now know what *not* to do. If you're not around, your chadults will have to reinvent the wheel every time. With your help, they can avoid unnecessary mistakes with that batch of problems, leaving them far more resources for tackling difficulties that are new to you as well as to them. In addition, there are uniquely grandmotherly services that only you can provide, services that will give them courage and confidence and joy they can't get any other way.

I can hear you thinking, "Oh, they'll never listen to *me!*" and "Oh, they'll do exactly the *opposite* of what I tell them!" Don't be too quick to leap to that conclusion. Those are two of the common annoyances that can be fixed by skillful grandmothering. There are ways of giving grown children—chadults—advice that will make that advice welcome and avoid a great deal of misery all around. I'll tell you about them as we go along.

❧ The Benefits for Your Grandchildren

To grandchildren today, a grandmother is often enormously important because she is the only stable element in a world of wildly shifting sands. This is just as true for families with plenty of money as it is for those who live from paycheck to paycheck or have no paycheck at all: *There are plenty of kinds of misery in today's world that aren't linked to money.* Every time we turn on the news we learn of another troubled person who's done some terrible thing—and who turns out to have had a hellish childhood. But when you look at a hundred people whose younger years were miserable, you'll find that among them there are survivors, people who were able to come through childhoods of torment and become fine adults. This isn't a matter of luck. From much careful scientific research, we've learned that what these survivors usually have in common is that as children they had at least one grown-up they could count on. Grandmothers have never been more desperately needed to fill that slot than they are now!

"What do you think about this new trend of grandparenting?"

🦋 The Benefits for Your Descendants

Today's families are forever on the move. They move from town to town, job to job, neighborhood to neighborhood, drastic change to drastic change. They need a history that will knit them together and prove to them that however incomprehensible life may be on any given day, they do belong to something. Grandmothers are uniquely equipped to make certain that what they belong to is a *family*. You don't want any of your descendants to have to fall back on belonging to a *gang*, for lack of any other resource.

🦋 The Benefits for You

Arthur Kornhaber, the "Dr. Spock of grandparenting," answers the question of what grandparents get from their role this way: "It gives meaning to their lives in a society that currently has no meaning for old age." That's true; and it is *more* true for grandmothers. Aging women are far less likely than their male counterparts to be viewed as "distinguished" or to be sought out and surrounded by admiring colleagues and protégés and potential romantic interests. And—because their lifespans are longer—they're much more likely to find themselves lonely or alone.

It's hard, at age forty or younger, to imagine finding yourself all alone. It may even sound like a delightful condition. When I (not very often) traveled on business as a young woman, my idea of a really splendid evening wasn't a whirl through the clubs and theaters and restaurants. It was room service—food fixed by somebody else and brought to me, and the resulting dirty dishes and leftovers taken away by somebody else—followed by an evening of blissful solitude during which I could do whatever I darn pleased. When your life is frantic and you live it in a crowd, as is true for so many busy mothers, that's how things look. But the time will come when the relatives and the friends and the colleagues that crowded your earlier life are gone. People move away; people go into nursing homes; people die. And there you are! That part of your life can be a dreary wasteland you drag yourself through or it can be full of love and joy—it's really up to you. Being a grandmother is one of the most reliable ways to guarantee the love and joy alternative.

Besides, you don't want some grandchild of your own remembering you in the future the way I remember my Grandmother Diana, do you?

🦋 The Benefits for Humankind

It's not an exaggeration to say that grandmothers might very well save this world from disaster. We keep hearing that everything's going to the dogs, that humanity is headed straight downhill and seems to be wallowing in its worst excesses, that civilization is falling apart all around us. Maybe this is nothing more than the usual fretting of older generations about things "not being like they used to be"; that's possible. On the other hand, there's a lot of evidence to indicate that the negative judgments are valid. And the people making them now include as many children and teenagers and young people as elderly adults.

Suppose it's true. Suppose we really are in serious trouble as a people and a planet. *If all the grandmothers help, there may still be time to fix it.* You never know. You might grandmother an Abraham Lincoln, an Eleanor Roosevelt, a Sojourner Truth. It's worth thinking about.

🦋 And What about the Grandfathers?

There's a book called *The Raging Granny Songbook*, in which a seven-year-old girl tells us that "a grandfather is a man grandmother." She has a point. Grandfathers are just as important as grandmothers. But books about grandfathering should be written *by* grandfathers, who are the experts on that subject.

I am confident that the grandfathers who read this book will have the wisdom to recognize all that is true in it for them, too, and will put it to good use.

❧ The Grandmother Principles

1. The grandmother way is the easy way.
2. Grandmothers already *have* tenure.
3. Everything comes to an end eventually.
4. A grandmother is a safe haven.
5. There's nothing so simple that you cannot make it complicated if you really try.
6. The most powerful way to teach is by example.
7. People with *real* clout don't *have* to throw their weight around.
8. Grandmothers don't *have* to be politically correct.
9. When getting somebody else to do a task is more work than just doing it yourself, do it yourself.
10. Most arguments are about who is in charge.
11. It's always *safe* to talk to a grandmother.
12. Grandmothers *delegate*.
13. A grandmother is not a quarterback.
14. *Somebody* has to be the grown-up.
15. No sickness or injury is so bad that panic can't make it a lot worse.
16. There are secret stories that only grandmothers should know.
17. It will be finished when it's finished.
18. Grandmothers plan for the long haul.
19. If it can't be done one way, it can be done some other way.
20. After you give people something, it belongs to *them*.
21. For grandmothers, the light doesn't have to be perfect.

Chapter 1

◘

Thinking Like a Grandmother

❧ The Grandmother Principles

Looking like a grandmother is no longer important the way it once was; times have changed. Not only do grandmothers in shorts no longer cause raised eyebrows, you really cannot tell much about a woman's generational status today just by her appearance. When I was a child, a woman who chanced to become a grandmother in her thirties felt obliged to make an immediate and drastic change in the way she dressed, in keeping with that new status. We're past that, thank goodness, and are free to focus on what really does matter, which is not your clothes but your mind. There are certain things about the way grandmothers *think* that are crucial to successful grandmothering.

No book could provide a list of every single thing a grandmother needs to know and do, even if all grandmothers were alike and every grandmother faced the same set of circumstances, which is clearly not the case. But that's all right. It's like golf, or cooking: once you've learned the basic rules and techniques, once you have the basic equipment, you can proceed no matter what golf course or kitchen you may have to deal with. Grandmother thinking is systems thinking, which is quite different from following a list. A system makes it possible to cope when something new comes at you; a list can only tell you how to handle the items written on it.

Every system has to be organized around a set of principles, and this one is no exception. The twenty-one Grandmother Principles (GPs, for short) presented in this book are guidelines that I have devel-

Uniforms

Much of my life I've envied nuns because they never had to worry about what to wear; I find it hard to understand why many orders of sisters have given up that advantage. Unless you're genuinely interested in fashion, I recommend that you choose some set of garments that can serve as a grandmother uniform and wear items from that set for every occasion. That way, your family knows that you'll always welcome a particular item, which is a plus; you can buy your things in quantity when they're on sale; and you'll never have to waste time fretting over how to dress. My own uniform is a pair of loose-fitting dark-colored slacks, a pullover sweater or shell, a loose shirt or jacket, and Birkenstocks.

"Louise, your outfit! You've gone retro!"

oped over a lifetime. You may find that you want to add to the set (in which case I'd be delighted if you'd share your additions with me, so that I can share them in turn with others). My GPs are based on common sense, long experience, and thorough testing in the real world. Some of them may come as a surprise to you; others will seem obvious. I can tell you confidently that following them will make your grandmothering more joyful, more useful, and less stressful. To introduce ourselves to grandmotherly thinking, let's begin by looking at the first four Grandmother Principles; we'll discuss them one at a time.

··

GRANDMOTHER PRINCIPLE 1:
THE GRANDMOTHER WAY IS THE EASY WAY.

··

For almost every human task, there are easy ways to do it and hard ways. Nongrandmothers often feel that they are required to do everything the hard way. Consider the plight of people who earn their living by giving lessons. They can't put food on their tables unless they stretch the process out into *lots* of lessons. Grandmothers are in a different situation; doing things the easy way is both their right and their privilege.

Nongrandmothers tend to believe that the easy way to do something is also the lazy way, or the crude way, or worse. Nongrandmothers in our culture have a strong need to feel that they are piling up accomplishments, establishing a track record of achievements, making a mark in the world, and proving that they're a force to be reckoned with. Grandmothers can and should set that way of thinking aside for good.

When you are a grandmother, you are no longer under any obligation to prove anything.

··

GRANDMOTHER PRINCIPLE 2:
GRANDMOTHERS ALREADY HAVE TENURE.

··

This doesn't mean that if you want to write a novel or compose a symphony or climb Mount Everest or breed a blue marigold you shouldn't go ahead and do it. Suppose you do win a Pulitzer Prize or discover a cure for ankylosing spondylitis—good for you! But you don't have to; it's not in your job description any longer.

There are women who've devoted their entire lives to leaping hurdles, women who after clearing each jump have always looked immediately for the next one, the one with an even higher bar. They will have to work actively at giving up that mindset. I have a dear friend, a writer (and grandmother) in her mid-eighties, who calls me now and then in great distress to say, "I don't know what's *wrong* with me! I can't seem to make myself go to my desk and *write!*" I explain to her that there's nothing wrong with her whatsoever and that if she doesn't feel like writing her customary five pages a day she doesn't have to. And she always sighs and says, "That's true, isn't it? I just needed to hear you say it one more time!" We need a rite of passage for grandmothers—some kind of solemn graduation ceremony.

Obviously, if you are a very young grandmother parts of this won't yet apply to you. Your schedule may be as heavy as ever; you may still have young children of your own at home; you may be holding down a full-time job. You may still have to get in there and write those five pages or weld those fifty widgets or whatever it is you regularly do. But you can't just dump grandmothering into that heavy schedule of yours and look upon it as only one more task that has to be completed, the way you could add thirty more widgets to be welded. You must instead start making adjustments in your life, the way you did when you became a mother. Grandmothering isn't just a new task; it's a new role. It may be hard for you to use the Grandmother Principles at your age, but it's not too early to start learning them and understanding them. It's much easier to hit a target when you know what you're aiming at.

....
GRANDMOTHER PRINCIPLE 3:
EVERYTHING COMES TO AN END EVENTUALLY.
....

Nongrandmothers tend to think that whatever is happening, good or bad, is going to keep right on happening. The younger they are, the more slowly time seems to pass for them. This undermines their sense of proportion and leads to melodrama.

Grandmothers hearing, "I will *never* be old enough to drive!" and "I'm *never* going to graduate from this stupid school!" and "This [whatever—pregnancy is a typical example] is *never* going to be over!" and "I will *never* love anybody else again!" know better. The time will go by; the course will be over; the despair or the ecstasy will pass and be replaced by a new despair or ecstasy.

When the younger members of your family are blissed out or distraught or panicked, it's important for you to be there with a solid understanding of this principle. People in despair and terror need to be able to turn to you and ask, "Will it ever end?" and get a calm "Absolutely. It always does" in response. People in ecstasy need to be able to ask, "If this doesn't go on forever, will I be able to bear it?" and get back a calm "Absolutely. You'll be fine." Even if they don't appear to be paying much attention to you at the time, they need to hear these messages. And they need to hear them from someone whose experience is substantial enough to serve as a foundation for such pronouncements.

There will be times so exceptionally "interesting" that you won't feel comfortable saying "Absolutely" because you realize you might turn out to be wrong. That happens once in a while. In such cases, pretending is unwise. The thing to say is, "I don't know for sure right this minute— but I expect to. As soon as I'm sure of the answer, I'll let you know." Not "If I'm ever sure" what the answer is, but "As soon as I'm sure."

....
GRANDMOTHER PRINCIPLE 4:
A GRANDMOTHER IS A SAFE HAVEN.
....

The one obligation that a grandmother does have is the one stated in this principle: the obligation to be a safe haven. Everything else in a young person's world today is likely to be in a state of uneasy fluctuation. Parents living in this tumult of ever faster and more sweeping change may seem to your grandchildren to be shifting and flowing, not secure enough themselves to be somebody to depend on. In times like these, grandmothers must offer *absolute consistency.*

You know how we all feel about McDonald's restaurants when we're on the road? That they are one unchanging place where we know that bathrooms will be clean, children will be welcome, and although the food won't be inspired it will be the same as it was last time you were at a McDonald's? As desert travelers once went from oasis to oasis, knowing they could count on drinkable water and at least one palm tree, we now go from McDonald's to McDonald's, feeling safe about doing that. Unromantic and unglamorous as it may seem, grandmothers need to be like that—in emotional terms. Never mind glamour, be consistent! It's far more important for you to maintain an image of absolute stability than any other image.

This doesn't mean that you, as grandmother, can never change. It just means that change should be carefully thought out, and—if it's a change that will be noticed—carefully explained. When my Grandmother Lewis turned sixty-five (which was considered very old in those days) she notified every household in the family that she would no longer be sending Christmas and birthday gifts. At that advanced age, she told us, and being a widow, it was simply too difficult. This was a big change; we had always looked forward to her generous and well-chosen gifts. But her action was consistent with everything we valued about her. It was logical, fair, and understandable; and once she'd announced it, we knew we could rely on it. She could have just stopped sending cards and gifts, or started sending them haphazardly or carelessly. She didn't do that. Her position was that if she could no longer do it in a way that met her personal standards she would not do it at all, and that her proper course was to explain that to us and be done with it.

And she *was* done with it. I point this out because I want to stress its importance. When Christmastime came around each year, she didn't begin a dreary lament about how sorry she was that she couldn't do the gift thing any longer, so that we all felt we had to start an equally dreary warble about how she mustn't worry about it and it didn't really matter.

She told us what was going to happen, it happened, and that was that. Which is as it should be.

Suppose you are a woman who has always had a very lackadaisical attitude about sending gifts, or a woman who has—perhaps for excellent reasons—never participated in family gift-giving in any way. That behavior will have become part of the family's image of you. They'll laugh when Christmas (or Hanukkah or Kwaanza or New Year's Day) goes by with no card or present from you, and they'll look at each other and say, "That's Grandma! You can count on her!" It would be just as unsettling to your family for you to suddenly change your ways without explanation as it would have been to mine if my grandmother had not done what she did.

When you make a change in your grandmothering, then, you want to do what you can to prepare everyone for it and fit it into people's lives by tying the new firmly to the old. Sometimes you can do that with a single statement at a family dinner. But often it's more complicated than that, or the announcement would spoil the dinner. Often the best way to do it is by mentioning the change in your *family newsletter,* several issues in a row, with an explanation and a series of progress reports.

A family newsletter is a good example of a technique for applying a number of Grandmother Principles at one time, efficiently and effectively. It's the easy way to do it. It's a way of demonstrating not only that everything comes to an end eventually, but also that that's normal and nothing to be alarmed about. And it's a way of being a safe haven. All at the same time. But how do you go about creating a family newsletter? I am just getting ready to tell you about that.

❧ The Family Newsletter

Things happen in families and take on a significance that no one outside the family could possibly understand. Unless someone is the designated rememberer, the time will come when people inside the family won't understand either. And there they'll all be—baffled! *Why did Grandmother Lewis never send a Christmas present to the youngest*

"When I was a child, my mother's mother told me it was for scaring dust out of the tepee."

grandchild? Why was the road between Uncle Jim's and Cousin Mario's farm called Sinner's Lane? Why is it important for men in your family to eat a bowl of pinto beans for breakfast on Father's Day? Nobody knows. *Why did Grandfather Lee refuse to speak to his sister for seventeen years, even though she lived across the street? Why did Great-Uncle Howard set the barn on fire?* Nobody knows. Nobody remembers.

People faced with puzzles like these tend to make things up. This is how a tale gets started that Grandmother Lewis thought red hair was a sign of wickedness and so, when her youngest grandchild was born a redhead, she never sent her a Christmas present. The truth is that

Grandmother Lewis never sent *anybody* a gift after she was sixty-five (and the youngest grandchild was born long after that); moreover, Grandmother Lewis was especially *fond* of redheads.

You don't have to let this happen, but you need the written word to prevent it. You can't be sure that you'll have a willing descendant to pass all the information along to orally, as happens in many traditional cultures. You can't be sure that at family gatherings there'll be people eager to hear you talk instead of watching the football game.

A family newsletter will solve these problems and is a wonderful ongoing gift that will be treasured—as long as you appear to do it effortlessly. If you appear to be working your fingers to the bone doing it, everyone will feel guilty, and then it will be a burden instead of a gift.

"Office" Supplies

Grandmothers need a lot of "office" supplies, even though they may not have an office. They need three-ring binders to keep family histories in (see pages 173–87) and make gifts with, they need big envelopes to mail things in, they need ordinary stationery, they need notebook paper—they need many things of this kind. Buying them one or two at a time makes them much too expensive. The way to buy such things is by mail (ordering by phone or fax if you like), from Quill Corporation; you can get a free catalog by calling (800) 789-6640. Quill will sell you very handsome three-ring binders for less than a dollar each if you buy a box of twelve; savings on everything else are comparable, and amazing. They also carry school supplies—crayons, colored markers, construction paper, stickers, and more. Quill pays the shipping on all orders over $45.00; if it's hard for you to put together an order that size, get some other grandmothers to help you in a combined order. (Twelve binders is not too many for anyone who has grandchildren.)

🦋 Writing the Newsletter

The first thing you do is take a cardboard box (or a roomy basket, or a very large envelope) and write "Newsletter Stuff" on it. Put it in a convenient spot, somewhere where you won't trip over it and other people won't rummage through it. Then start throwing newsletter material in there as you come across it or as it occurs to you.

Don't set up a fancy filing system. You don't need one. It's not the *New York Times*. Anything that you'd write about in a letter to your family goes in that box, until you have enough to fill a few pages. (Six pages is a good maximum size, because you can mail six sheets of paper in a regular business envelope for one stamp and still tuck in a personal note or a cereal coupon or a snapshot.)

While the material is piling up, sit down and design your first issue. Here's a sample design, with comments, to get you started and show you how easy it is to do.

THE SMITH FAMILY IRREGULAR
Issue #1, December 1999

[The word *irregular* in the newsletter's name is an important part of doing this the easy way. It lets you bring out each issue when you have enough material on hand to make it interesting. It doesn't commit you to any kind of schedule, which means that when you don't feel like doing an issue you can put it off without disappointing anybody, including yourself.]

🦋 WHAT'S HAPPENING

[Here you put all the news you're willing to print. News about yourself and your activities, items you've gathered about others in the family and about people you know your family would be interested in—close friends, teachers, and so on. If you write pleasant, chatty letters easily, model this section on your usual letter. If not, get a copy of a newspaper from any small town and read the local news column—the one about

who visited and who had a party and who's sick and who had a baby—
and use that as a model.]

❦ THINGS TO REMEMBER

[Here you put important dates coming up, like graduations and birthdays and anniversaries and trips. If you have absentminded family members, this is the place to put a reminder that it's time to check their propane tanks or do their taxes. This is where you put a note that fourteen-year-old Anne will be singing a solo in church next week. It's also the best spot for a reminder that the family promised you somebody would come put up your storm windows by September 10th.]

❦ A FAMILY STORY FOR YOUR COLLECTION

[Here you put the story that *explains* why the Smith men are supposed to eat a bowl of pinto beans for breakfast on Father's Day, just as you'd tell it if you were talking and had a willing audience.]

❦ ANNOUNCEMENTS FROM YOUR EDITOR

[This is the spot for your own announcements when they are more serious than those you put into the "What's Happening" section. Here is where you announce, for instance, that you've decided it's time for your various chadults to start hosting the big Thanksgiving Day dinner instead of you, and that you want them to take turns, starting with whichever one strikes you as the best first choice for that task—and this is where you explain why.

This is also the perfect spot come the day you want to tell your family something like this:

> I want all of you to know that I have decided to go away for two weeks, from January 9th to 23rd. I have a very good reason for going, I assure you. I don't intend to tell you what the reason is; you'll just have to trust me this time. And I know I can count on you not to let my water pipes freeze while I'm away.

If you've been doing this right all along, they *will* trust you, they won't pester you to explain, and they will look after your water pipes.]

🦋 MISCELLANEOUS
[Here you put a quotation or joke you think everybody would enjoy, a recipe or a good craft idea, a book you'd like to recommend, or anything else you'd like to pass along that doesn't fit anywhere else.]

🦋 THE END
Let the Newsletter Stuff box fill up and don't worry about it until it's full enough. When it is, dump the contents out on the floor or anywhere else that's convenient and sort it into piles according to your newsletter design. A pile for "What's Happening," a pile for "Miscellaneous," and so forth. Then write your first issue as outlined above or according to your own fancy, keeping firmly in mind that it's *your* newsletter, you're in charge of it, and nobody is going to give you a grade on it. A grandmother's family newsletter has two purposes:

❖ To help you knit the family together, even if they're widely scattered around the world, even if they rarely have a chance to meet.
❖ To provide you with a way to get information out to family members promptly and accurately, at your own convenience, in your own style, and without being interrupted or contradicted.

The hard part is getting that first issue done, and the grandmotherly way to do it doesn't involve writing a sentence, looking at it critically, throwing it away and writing it again, looking at it critically another time, and so on, ad infinitum. *Just get a first draft finished.* That's what I do, even if I'm writing a whole book. Once you have a draft in front of you (and if you're working on the computer, that means a printed-out draft), the newsletter exists as a physical object in the real world. You can then look it over and do any fooling about with it that strikes you as necessary. Gustave Flaubert, the man who wrote *Madame Bovary,* was famous for the agonizing care he took with every sentence; he was happy if he could write one finished paragraph a day. That's fine for young French authors; it's not appropriate for grandmothers doing newsletters.

❧ Producing the Newsletter

If you're a grandmother who is at ease with computers and printers, you know exactly what to do next. Type up issue no. 1, print out a copy for your files and one for each household in your family, put the copies in envelopes, and mail them out. If computers aren't your thing, that's not a problem: type your first issue or write it out in longhand, whichever you prefer, make copies on your own copier or have them run off at a local copy center, put the copies in envelopes, and mail them out.

Gifts from Your Copy Machine

The combination of a copy machine and a three-ring binder will let you make gifts of many many kinds, easily. Do you have a grandson who's crazy about everything Native American? A granddaughter who dotes on butterflies? A grandchild whose hero is a particular sports star or rock musician? Make the child a notebook full of copies of articles and pictures and information on the chosen subject. Unlike just buying a book, you can tailor your binder exactly to the child's interests and abilities. And you and the child can add new items over time to make the binder even more wonderful and valuable. You can also make notebooks of family photographs, on as narrow or broad a subject as you wish, with comments and explanations added; today even small copiers can be set to make good, clear black-and-white copies of photographs. You can make binders full of jokes, or stories, or letters, or recipes, or craft ideas. . . . The possibilities are unlimited, and these are very special gifts that will be treasured.

Either way, copies that are punched for a three-ring binder are a good idea. Punched copies will encourage your family to keep them in a notebook, where they're less likely to get lost. That way, when one of your kids suddenly remembers that there was something in the last newsletter about your storm windows, he or she will know where to look for details.

And that's issue no. 1. From then on, your newsletter will be simplicity itself.

While we're on the subject, I want to tell you that I consider a copying machine of your own to be the most useful grandmothering tool since the invention of the diaper. Many tasks that are otherwise horribly difficult become minor matters if you have a reasonably good copier of your own. The variety of wonderful presents you can put together quickly and for almost no money with a copier will amaze you. The next time all your kids and grandkids start asking you what you want for your birthday or other gift event, I strongly recommend telling them to pool their resources and get you a reliable small copying machine, with ample supplies included. And tell them that on future such occasions you'd rather have more supplies and a paid-up service contract for the copier than another silk scarf or pair of earrings.

Certain objections may well have crossed your mind as you were reading this section. Let me answer the four most likely ones before we go on.

❖ "But that's an incredible amount of work!"

I assure you, it's not. Like so many things, the first time is the hardest.

....

GRANDMOTHER PRINCIPLE 5:
THERE'S NOTHING SO SIMPLE THAT YOU CANNOT
MAKE IT COMPLICATED IF YOU REALLY TRY.
....

It's possible to make this hard, too, but you'd really have to work at it. Resist the temptation to do that. Protests along the lines of "But I don't

Leaving Nobody Out

When you have a big family, it's hard to keep track of who you've done what for lately. The easy way is to make a chart with every family member's name on it and run off a batch of copies. Then—supposing you're including a personal note to one family member each time you mail out your newsletter, or you're sending prints of photographs from some occasion and don't want to send them all at the same time—you write what you're doing across the top of the page and cross out each name as you attend to it.

know how to write" and "But I'd make grammar mistakes" are for young people worried about What People Will Think; grandmothers don't have to concern themselves with such things.

A newsletter like this saves vast amounts of your time and energy —many, many times the amount that you put into creating it—because it lets you get necessary family business *done.* Instead of being inter-rupted every sentence or two as you try to talk, instead of having to worry that Ellen will be embarrassed and Fiona will be angry, instead of having to figure out how to keep Jack from starting a fight with Margery over your third important point—you just do it. All family members read their own copy in private and can react to it in private, with plenty of time to calm down about it before anyone else is in-volved. It's wonderful.

❖ "But nobody in my family would *read* it!"

Once again, that's false. They may not be willing to admit that they read it, but they will discover that it's a big help to have it available, and they *will* read it. They will also read it to find out what you've said about them personally. And as they grow older themselves and begin to gain some wisdom about family bonds, they will read it with great pleasure.

❖ "But they'll make fun of it and say it's stupid!"

If so, that's *their* problem and not worth two minutes of your time and energy. Such behavior indicates a bad case of either immaturity, which will be outgrown, or jealousy because the individuals doing the mocking wish *they* had thought of it instead of you. As long as it serves the two purposes I listed on page 36 for you, this is absolutely irrelevant.

❖ "But it's so impersonal!"

Every time you send out an issue, tuck something extra into just one envelope, until you've done that for everybody, at which point you start over with the person who was first. Include a little personal note, a photograph, a stamp for somebody's collection, a cartoon with a Post-It saying, "I saw this and I knew you'd get a kick out of it." Something simple but meaningful for the person you send it to. That will be enough to keep the whole project from being impersonal, and it's an easy way to maintain ties with everyone in your family at the same time. You finish off two (and maybe several) birds this way, with only one stone!

🎔 The Family Role Model

Grandmothers, even quite young ones, quickly discover that they have a store of experience and wisdom that would solve a multitude of problems—if only they could magically insert it into the minds of their children and grandchildren. But since magic is in such short supply, how, they wonder, can they share what they know? The family newsletter is a good start, but it can't do it all.

Nongrandmothers tend to believe that knowledge should be transferred by direct instruction, the way teachers transfer their knowledge of long division. But grandmothers, taking a longer view and seeing a larger picture, think about this differently. They know that although direct instruction within a family is sometimes necessary, it breeds resistance that gets in the way of learning—especially when nobody requested it. Whenever it can be avoided, there's a better way.

GRANDMOTHER PRINCIPLE 6:
THE MOST POWERFUL WAY TO TEACH IS BY EXAMPLE.

When you are the most stable element in your family's world, chances are high that you will be a role model for your grandchildren, even—as far as character is concerned—for your grandsons. Your chadults, fond as they are of you, will probably perceive you as they always have. Until they're out of their twenties, if not their thirties, that may not be a flattering image. But your grandchildren see you differently. Unlike their parents, they didn't grow up thinking of you as the only barrier standing between them and Everything They Ever Wanted

"Mother, sometimes you're worse than the kids."

To Do. Given half a chance they will look up to you and want to be like you, without any negative preconceptions.

This opportunity to be a role model is a privilege and a blessing. It lets you offer an alternative to such competing role models as Barbie, neighborhood drug dealers, the latest eighty-five-pound supermodels, and rock stars who set their guitars afire on stage. Be grateful for it! However, as is true of all privileges, it carries its share of responsibilities.

No matter which of the four basic grandmother types you've chosen for yourself (see pages 15–19), there are three kinds of grandmother role models that you should do your best to avoid: the Commander in Chief (CIC), the Full Professor, and the Martyr. They can be very tempting, but none of them will bring you anything but grief.

🦋 Not Being a Commander in Chief

Some grandmothers consider it their right and/or obligation to try to run their extended family like a military unit, controlling every breath drawn and every breath exhaled. They say things like these:

- ❖ "Don't be ridiculous! No one in our family has ever married a lion tamer and you're not going to be the first!" It is one of the predictable characteristics of the CIC-role-model grandmothers that a high percentage of their utterances begin with "Don't be ridiculous," "Don't be absurd," and "Don't be stupid."
- ❖ "You're not going out looking like that, and that's final." It's equally predictable that a high percentage of their utterances end with "and that's final," "and I don't want to hear another word from you about it," and "case closed."

One of my children's grandmothers chose the CIC model and was highly skilled at it. She would send me back to change what I was wearing, over and over again, until I hit on something she felt she could tolerate. It wasn't an endearing habit. It was of course ridiculous—and absurd and stupid—for me to go along with it. But I was very young, and I had no idea how to deal with such behavior.

It may be that everything runs smoothly in your family, in the capable hands of trustworthy and competent adults. If so, I congratulate you; you need only relax and watch them with love and pride. You not only don't need to issue any orders in that enviable circumstance, but it would be a waste of your resources if you did, and inappropriate as well.

But suppose that members of your family really and truly are so inept and incompetent that unless *you* run things life will be an endless string of disasters. Many books about family relationships will tell you that that's not possible. They'll tell you that when you feel that way it's only evidence that you're unwilling to let your children grow up. The books are wrong. It most certainly is possible for your progeny to be just as clueless as you think they are, especially if they're very young and inexperienced. When that's your situation—even when cases of Disaster-Prone Syndrome are mild—there are two things you have to learn to do.

❖ Let them make as many mistakes as you possibly can. This isn't easy. It means standing by while they run into walls and fall out of trees. It takes a cool head and good judgment, qualities that go with thinking like a grandmother but don't necessarily come naturally.

❖ Keep your iron fist hidden in a velvet glove when you absolutely must take charge. This isn't easy either; I won't pretend it is. It means always thinking before you speak, it means refraining from saying many unpleasant and well-deserved truths, and it takes a lot of self-discipline.

As difficult as they may be, these two strategies are the only way to go. Not because they're "nice" (although I suspect Miss Manners would approve) but because otherwise your children and grandchildren will never grow out of their dependence on you, and that's not good. Think about it. You're not immortal. When you die, who will look after them?

Secondhand Discipline

One of the surest ways to create permanent resentment and bad feeling in your family is to discipline your chadults for your grandchildren's behavior—please don't do it. For example, suppose you think the grandkids should send you thank-you notes for gifts. Tell the *grandkids* so, not their parents! You can tell your chadults once, on the off chance that they might say, "You're right, Mother, they should do that—I just hadn't thought of it." But after that one mention, if you feel that you must complain, complain directly to the grandchildren.

I'll provide you with a generous supply of Velvet Glove translations in this book. For example, the Velvet Glove version of many "Don't be ridiculous" utterances goes like this: "I knew a person who tried that once, and the results were really dreadful. I wonder if there's something else you could do instead. What do *you* think?"

Grandmothers may command and sometimes must command, but they should never throw their weight around. It's their responsibility as role models to demonstrate Grandmother Principle 7:

GRANDMOTHER PRINCIPLE 7:
PEOPLE WITH *REAL* CLOUT DON'T *HAVE* TO
THROW THEIR WEIGHT AROUND.

🦋 Not Being a Full Professor

Nothing is more tiresome than a person who always behaves as if she knows everything about every subject and has the right to give grades in it. You want to be the person to whom people say, "Grandmother (or Mother), do you know anything about mutual funds?" who answers, "A little bit. Shall I tell you what I know?" and who gets a willing "Yes, please!" in reply. That won't happen if you constantly play out scenes like this one:

> X: Maybe we ought to *drive* to Arkansas.
> You: It's a terrible drive. It takes six hours, there's nowhere to eat along the way, and everybody in southern Missouri drives like a maniac.
> X: Oh. Well . . . it was just a thought.
> You: People your age are always confusing wild ideas with actual thinking. It's a dangerous and destructive tendency, and it can lead to catastrophes. That's why so many more accidents happen to young people.
> X: Oh.

When you know a great deal, the temptation to share it by force is strong. Resist! Except when *invited* to lecture, and in actual emergencies.

🦋 Not Being a Martyr

Many of the things that people ask grandmothers to do are a tad tedious; some are downright unpleasant. The rewards for doing them are often ample compensation—trust me—but at the time you're actually doing them you will be thinking what a drag they are. It would be nice if just getting them done, never mind how, were enough. But this is the real world, and it's not like that. When you are asked to do things you don't want to do, *either do them graciously or don't do them at all.* It's far better to refuse than to be a Martyr, modeling Martyr behavior for all the young people around you to observe and learn from.

Suppose you've been asked to stay home and look after the grand-kids while their parents go out to dinner to celebrate some occasion, and you'd much rather not. You have three appropriate choices for responding to that request:

1. "Of course I will—I'd be glad to. What time do you need me to be there?" (Graciously. Sincerely.)
2. "No, dear. Not tonight." (Or "Not Tuesday night." Or "Not until fall." Or whatever fits your circumstances, including, "No, dear. Never.")
3. "I won't do that, but I'll make you a counteroffer. I'll pay for a sitter, and you can call that my contribution to your celebration."

The following response—the Martyr one—is never appropriate and should be avoided like chicken pox: "Of *course* I will, I'd *love* to! You know me—I'll just make do with whatever leftovers you've got in the refrigerator! You two just run along and have a wonderful time! Don't think about *me* at *all!* Okay? *I'll* be all right; I'm *used* to sitting around by myself with nothing to do."

It's okay to say no. That's every grandmother's privilege. It's not okay to say yes and charge for your services in guilt.

For some women, thinking like a grandmother is relatively easy, perhaps because they were fortunate enough to have had a grandmother whose example taught them how it's done. All they have to do is shift gears. For other women it can mean looking at the world and everything in it in a way that may be very new and strange. In either case, the benefits will always be worth the investment.

🦋 If You're a "Long-Distance" Grandmother

You can still do the family newsletter, even though it will be of little use to you for such things as getting someone in the family to stop by your place and do minor errands. But because you're not close by, the newsletter may be even more vital to the task of tying the family together.

You can always use the telephone, whether you're one mile or one thousand miles away. When you phone your grandchildren, however, you want to be able to talk with them and feel as though all of you are enjoying the experience. That won't happen if the child is jumping up and down with eagerness to leave for the swimming pool; it won't happen if the child was in the middle of an exciting game with friends when the phone rang and had to be ordered to come inside and talk to you. The way to be sure your calls to your grandkids are a success is to call *by appointment.* Write a note or send an e-mail message (or make a

Electronic Grandmothering

Unless the very thought of a computer gives you the jitters, do get one—and a modem—so that you can communicate with your children and grandchildren (and your online friends) by e-mail. Even if you do nothing but e-mail, you'll get your money's worth from this resource, and you'll probably find that as you get used to electronic grandmothering you'll want to do many other things as well. For example, you'll want to go to the multitude of Web sites where free grandparenting resources of every kind are offered. (You'll find the addresses of a number of these sites listed on page 93.)

Have someone who knows all about these things help you choose your equipment, set it up, arrange for Internet access, and get you started, no matter how "user-friendly" a salesperson tells you products are. In the long run this will save you far more than it costs. (You may find that your grandchildren can do it with ease, for free.) If you spend your first six weeks of electronic grandmothering in a state of constant misery because nothing seems to work, you'll end up hating the whole thing. Don't let that happen—get help.

"Every time I get an A my Grandma puts it on her Web site."

very *brief* call) asking when would be a good time for a telephone chat, and agree on a day and time for it. (I would advise making phone appointments with the chadults as well, if you want to talk to them for more than just a few minutes.) It's lovely to be spontaneous and surprise people, but telephone calls aren't an appropriate vehicle; all too often they are such inconvenient interruptions that they cause nothing but resentment. Even if your family is polite and claims that it's not necessary, scheduling calls in advance is the wise way to go. And any time you make an unexpected call that's not for an emergency, your first line should be something like, "Is this a good time to talk?" so that the person on the other end of the phone has a window of opportunity for letting you know, without being rude, that it's not.

Send a regular letter or card or e-mail to your grandkids. Once a month is okay, or at the beginning of each season of the year. As with your phone calls, don't make it a surprise. You want your grandchildren to be able to depend on your communication with them. When your grandmothering has to be done at a distance you have no reliable way of knowing about the crises in their lives and the times when even a short message from you would be a badly needed source of comfort and strength.

Get a copy of Selma Wasserman's wonderful book *The Long Distance Grandmother: How to Stay Close to Distant Grandchildren.* It's packed with information and ideas; you'll find it indispensable.

You might also want to consider getting one of the units that lets you surf the Internet, and both send and receive e-mail, *without* a computer, using your television set and a cordless keyboard; this is much less expensive and complicated than a full computer setup. There are various brands. A very nice and reasonably priced unit is the one offered by the WebTV Network; for information, call 1 (800) GOWEBTV (469-3288).

◘

Chapter 2

Nudging, Nagging, and Nattering— Do You Have To?

I'm sure that some of the unease many women feel when they learn that they're about to become grandmothers comes from a common stereotype about grandmotherly communication. That stereotype portrays grandmothers—already perceived as "old"—as women who nag and complain and whine and carry on, scarcely able to get through the simplest exchange without interfering in the lives of others. Certainly there are grandmothers like that, but there are women and men of all ages who behave that way, and grandmothers are no more likely to than anyone else. The stereotype needs to be plucked out of our collective consciousness the way you'd remove a noxious bug from a prize rosebush. It's true that grandmothers often find themselves involved in complicated communication maneuvers within a family; it's *not* true that they can only carry out these maneuvers in a way that makes everyone around them dread their very presence. In fact, a grandmother's unique position and circumstances usually give her a freedom to *avoid* unpleasant communication that she has never had before.

"When Grandma says she's gay, she means she's feeling happy."

🦋 Thinking Like a Grandmother

When you yourself are a parent of young children and teenagers, you're up against a cold, hard fact: *You can't always be nice.* You may be the world's most liberal person, you may have a deep distaste for taking charge—it makes no difference. As long as you have primary responsibility for the behavior of youngsters of your own, you have to spend a lot of time telling them what to do and leaning on them until they do it. Because young parents are new at that, most of them learn it "on the job," making lots of mistakes as they bumble along. It's amazing that first children (and only children) ever turn out to be satisfactory people, considering.

Grandmothers (except those who are in the difficult position of filling in as full-time caregivers for grandkids) are in a very different situation. Not only are they not directly answerable for the grandchildren's behavior, they have no control over it at all. Suppose you have always made your children clean their plates, and now your daughter lets your grandchildren leave anything they don't like, uneaten. Face it:

there's nothing you can do about it. Unless your chadults' care of their kids is literally abusive or puts the children in genuine danger (in which case you have to call in outside help), it's out of your control. You can give advice, you can make suggestions, but the parents have the final say. This leaves you with two choices.

You can let the situation drive you crazy, wasting vast amounts of energy fretting about it or, worse still, struggling against it. *This will guarantee constant tension and stress,* either in your personal life, as you —in Martyr mode—suffer in silence and agonize over your helplessness and its terrible consequences, or in your interactions with your family, which—with you as Commander in Chief or Full Professor—will take on all the warmth and charm of the front lines in a combat zone. Alternatively, you can accept the situation and use your energy in more useful ways. I assure you, the second choice is the one to go for.

By the time you become a grandmother, you will know that there are many ways of getting people to do things that are more satisfactory than giving orders or begging. You will know that stories and metaphors have more power than direct commands or passionate pleas. You will know that people, including your most difficult relatives, are basically good, and if given a chance will do their best to please. (Which means that children who are constantly told, "You're stupid, you can't do anything right, you'll never amount to anything, you're a loser," will do their best to live up to those claims.) And grandmothers know that in all these things the problem is not general wickedness but *pride* and its partner, *shame.* All that knowledge is immensely valuable and should be shared with those you love. But just lecturing about it is useless. You have to use other methods.

❧ Getting People to Do Things They're Afraid to Do

People who are afraid don't do well, and they often don't think clearly. People can get to be sixty years old and look back at their lives and realize that they've never done anything much, just because they were always afraid of what might happen. It's a blessing that young human beings are too ignorant of what raising a family is like to know they should be scared; otherwise the human race would have died out long ago!

As a foundation for all other communication, grandmothers need to get two messages across to their grandchildren (and often to the parents of their grandchildren as well):

1. No matter what happens, you will always love them.
2. No matter what messages they're getting out in the world, it's not shameful to fail and it's not shameful to lose. It's only shameful not to *try*.

Watch a baby trying to learn to walk. It doesn't worry about what might happen. It doesn't worry about what people will think. It doesn't worry about how it will look to others as it struggles with the task. It doesn't give up and just lie there. It gets up and falls down and gets up and falls down and gets up again, patiently, doggedly, until the job is done. It takes some babies longer than others, and some babies take more falls than others, but all babies who are not gravely disabled learn to walk. We have no better model for getting ahead in this world than the one that every baby sets before us in this way, day after day after day.

When one of the family comes to you and says straight out, "I'm scared. What should I do?" that's a gift. It's a credit to your grandmothering. When that happens, you can just sit down and offer your best advice in the most loving way you know. Acknowledge the possible dangers; discuss the hazards for as long as is necessary to make them clear and weigh them carefully; and then help in the hard process of making a decision.

Much of the time, however, it won't happen that way. Instead of the truth, there will be bluster and defiance and a thousand invented explanations. And you will be tempted to say, "That's all nonsense! You're just scared." Don't do it. Resist that temptation. Forcing someone to admit fear will shame that person, and shame is the enemy. You have two far better alternatives: story telling and listening. They work together, and should both be used, in whatever order serves your needs.

Suppose your grandson, reminded to study for a math test, flatly refuses, and says, "I don't care about that stupid test! Math is dumb! Everybody knows that! I'm gonna play football! I don't need stupid math, it's a waste of my time!" The child's parents and teachers will take care of telling him what nonsense that is and ordering him to march himself off to study whether he thinks it's dumb or not. Now what?

If the child is willing to listen to you, tell a story: "When I was little, I was scared of math tests. I was so scared that one time I . . ."

Metaphor Power—the Language Traffic Rules

Just telling children how they should do things is often pretty much a waste of time. But giving them the same information in the form of a *metaphor* can produce amazing results. The best metaphor for teaching them how to carry on a conversation is LANGUAGE IS TRAFFIC. Tell them that human beings use cars to move people and pets and things from place to place, and unless they follow a set of traffic rules for doing that it doesn't work— they have crashes. In the same way, human beings use language to move information from person to person, and they have to have traffic rules or it can't be done. Don't tell them it's not nice to interrupt; tell them that interrupting somebody is like not waiting for your turn to go through a traffic light. Don't tell them it's rude to change the subject abruptly; tell them that it's like changing lanes without signaling. When they commit some conversational offense, ask them, "Suppose you were driving a car and you did that. What do you think would happen?" Metaphors (which are just bouillon-cubed stories) are powerful; a child who understands one will be able to expand it and extend it to new and different circumstances.

Or "When your daddy was little, he was scared of math tests. He was so scared that one time he . . ." Or "That reminds me of a story. Once there was a boy who was really scared of math tests. He was so scared that one time he . . ."

Never "He was scared of math tests, too" or "I was scared of math tests just like you are." You don't want to say anything that accuses the child of being scared. You're just saying, "As long as we're talking about math tests . . . while we're here . . . let me tell you how I felt about them." The child may be willing then, at the end of the story, to say, "You know what? I'm scared, too." And then it would be possible to talk about that fear, and perhaps to help with the problem.

If the child isn't willing to listen, *you* begin by listening. Say, "What happened the last time you took one of those tests? How was it? How did it go?" And then listen, with your full attention and without interrupting, until the child is willing to give you a turn.

You'll hear people say that it's useless to ask kids to talk to you about things. They'll bring up the classic example:

"How was school?"
"Okay."
"What did you do?"
"Nothing."

But suppose you have always, from the very begining, demonstrated to your grandchildren that you're willing to have real conversations with them. Conversations in which you give them the same consideration you would give adults. Conversations in which you follow the language traffic rules—*stay in your own lane, don't cut other people off, don't hog the road*—just as you would in talking with adults. In that case, the classic communication breakdown won't occur. Some children are more talkative than others, sure. But kids only insist on that "Okay/Nothing" routine when their attempts at conversation are always met with ridicule or annoyance or a barrage of questions or "Don't bother me, dear, I'm busy."

"Dear, I hope you don't think I'm too old-fashioned, but do you think you could call me 'Grandmother' or 'Grandma' instead of 'Butt-Head'?"

As a grandmother, you really can give your grandchildren a chance to learn how to carry on conversations with others—one of the most important skills for getting ahead in this world and being happy in it. Parents may be too busy or too worried to do this; teachers may have so many youngsters to oversee that it's impossible for them to do it. The days when every family sat down together at meals and talked, the days when they sat outside on the porch in the evening and had conversations, are long gone. Many of our children are growing up today with no model for conversation except the way they see people talk to each other on television. Grandmothers are in a position to do something about this problem, which is every bit as serious, every bit as dangerous for the children and for our society as the much more publicized "literacy crisis." If you're a long-distance grandmother, you may have to provide much of the conversation experience by telephone. That's fine; it's no less valuable.

And however things go in your conversations, always remember: Make sure the child goes away knowing that your love can be counted on absolutely, *no matter what,* and that the only shame is in refusing to try.

🦋 Getting People to Do Things They're Unwilling to Do

Suppose your family is having a formal reception as part of a wedding and your teenage grandchild refuses to put on conventional clothes for the occasion. She'll go, she says, but she's going to wear her usual baggy shorts and tank top and sneakers and Hair-from-Mars.

You can fix this by giving an order only in the rare case when what she needs is an *excuse* for doing something and your direct order will provide her with that excuse: "The only reason I'm wearing these nerdy clothes is because my grandmother *ordered* me to!" Otherwise, commanding her to dress conventionally will only make her dig in her heels harder.

You can't fix it by begging: "Please, honey, do it for Grandma!" or "If you really loved your Grandma, you'd do it!" You can't fix it by bribing: "If you'll put on a dress and do your hair decently, just this once, I'll buy you those earrings you've been wanting for so long." *Grandmothers absolutely must not do those things, because they would stand as proof that you're just as helpless against bad behavior as anybody else.* Grandchildren badly need to know that that's not the case!

Begin by listening, with your full attention, while the child tells you why she is right to do what she plans to do. Don't interrupt her, don't rush her. Say "Hmmmmm" and "I see" and "Really," and let it all go by, no matter how ridiculous it may get, until she's exhausted. Next, tell the story that you have ready for just such situations (see pages 158–72). And if none of that has any effect, try this:

> *You:* All right, you've convinced me. Maybe you're right. But now I need your help.
>
> *Child:* (Warily) You need my help . . . like how?
>
> *You:* I'm going to try it your way, dear. Dress like you, I mean. But you have to go with me to buy an outfit like yours, because I don't have a clue what to get.
>
> *Child:* You mean you'd go to the reception dressed like *me?*

You: Right. No more stupid dresses. No more stupid high-heeled shoes. Let's do it. What time can you go to the mall with me?

Child: Grandmother! You can't be *serious!*

You: I have to go pick it out without your help, then?

Child: Grandmother, listen to me . . . Old people don't dress like that!

You: Well, I don't see why not. If you've got the courage to do it, so do I. I'll just follow your lead.

This is a perfect example of the need for grandmothers to be absolutely consistent and always keep their word. The reason it will work, and will get your granddaughter to the reception properly dressed, is that she can be certain that if you say you'll go to that occasion in sneakers and baggy pants and a tank top and Hair-from-Mars, just like her, you can be counted on to follow through. The dialogue should end like this:

Child: All right, Grandma. I'll put on a dress and do my hair. I'll even wear regular shoes.

You: You're sure?

Child: I'm sure.

You: You can tell people, "I'm only dressed like this because my grandmother had a hissy fit." I'll be glad to take the heat. Will that help?

Child: Yeah, a little. You'll back me up?

You: Why not? I *did* have a hissy fit. There are lots of different kinds of hissy fits.

(If this doesn't work, and you have to go through with your offer, that's not all bad. Just think what a fabulous story it will add to your family collection!)

Obviously, grandchildren (and chadults) are sure to declare their intention to do all kinds of things that you can't or shouldn't offer to do right along with them. I realize that. But the basic strategy outlined above, ready for tailoring to your specific set of circumstances, will be clear. When all else fails, look for something you can offer to do that you're reasonably confident will be turned down—but that you're prepared to actually do if the unexpected happens and it's accepted. It should be something that is truly an offer, not a threat; something that will break through an impasse and make it possible for the resistant child to give in gracefully. Nongrandmothers—most of them younger than you, afflicted with pride and worried to death about their image—can't afford to make such offers. Grandmothers can, and they should.

❧ Dealing with People Who Have Had to Do Things They Were Afraid or Unwilling to Do

People who've come out on the short end of a disagreement are already feeling one or more points down. Letting them feel that way is penalty enough. Adding to it by rubbing their noses in it is a sure way to make them determined never to change their minds for you again, even if they'd like to. You want to avoid that in every way possible.

Never say any of the following things to people who had to do something that they feared or were opposed to doing.

"See? I was *right!*"
"Maybe next time you'll listen to me sooner!"
"See how much better things go when you listen to me?"
"Aren't you glad you listened to me?"
"Aren't you sorry you were so stubborn?"
"Look how things turned out! I told you so, didn't I?"
"Now don't you feel better about this since you've stopped
      being so stubborn?"
"Now aren't you glad you changed your mind?"

As a general guideline for grandmothering, I urge you to avoid completely all negative questions—that is, questions starting with "Don't you . . ." "Didn't you . . ." "Aren't you . . ." "Can't you . . ." and so on. They carry an obnoxious message that says, "I already know the answer to the question I'm asking, but I insist on asking it anyway and demand that you answer it, for your own good." If you really need to find out whether someone is sorry, "Are you sorry?" will get the answer for you just as efficiently as "Aren't you sorry?" without dragging in all the counterproductive negatives.

People who must do something unwillingly, whether because of fear or disagreement or for any other reason, are fragile and vulnerable, at least until it's over and settled. The more they perceive themselves as persecuted underdogs (as most adolescents do, for example, and as many middle children do), the more true that will be. Be aware of that, and do nothing to take advantage of it. And then, down the road, you may well be rewarded with, "I'm really glad now that you convinced me to go ahead and do that! Thanks, Grandma!" (Or "Thanks, Mom.")

❧ Knowing When to Give Up

One of the burdens young people struggle under is a conviction that giving up is *never* allowed, no matter how totally absurd it is to go on. It's particularly infuriating to watch the results of this idea when they hate what they've decided to do and would love to change their minds, and everybody else wants them to change their minds, but they're more afraid of damage to their pride than they are of the consequences of sticking to their original decision.

Their attitude is understandable. After all, you've told them again and again that they must keep trying, like the babies learning to walk mentioned earlier. After all, there are true stories of people who kept trying long after everyone had told them they were out of their minds, long after all the evidence seemed to bear that out, and who turned out to be right. That does happen. Nevertheless, there usually comes a point when trying has gone on long enough and quitting is both justified and admirable. Knowing exactly where that point is takes wisdom and experience, and grandmothers are often the right people to make the judgment. Like this:

You: Honey, you've really tried. You've tried your very best. You've proved that you're not a quitter. It's okay to stop now and just say that it didn't work.

   X: Are you sure?

You: I'm positive.

When what your grandchild or chadult is struggling to do is something of major significance—finding a solution for global warming, developing a corn plant that will grow in salt water, becoming the governor of the state, selling a first novel, finishing a Ph.D. in mathematics, getting on an Olympic team—it makes sense for them to hang in there until failure cannot possibly be avoided. But it makes *no* sense to use that strategy when the grim dedication is to something routine or even trivial (and it usually is). Whatever it is, it won't seem trivial to the determined individuals involved; they're too close to it and have invested in it too heavily. You don't ever want to *tell* them it's routine or trivial. Just tell them it's okay to give up now.

And you should show yourself the same courtesy, by the way. If you have tried your very best, over and over and over, to turn some feckless grandchild into a responsible person—to no avail—it's okay to give up. It's okay to decide that you love that child and will always love that child, but that you don't intend to spend any more energy on the hopeless project of trying to *change* that child.

Suppose one of your grandchildren had a severe physical disability. You'd see that everything possible was done to help. And then the time would come when you'd have to accept the fact that that child would never run or dance or climb trees. You wouldn't feel obligated to keep trying to force the child to do the impossible, and you wouldn't love the child any less. Exactly the same thing holds for the child whose handicap is emotional or spiritual. You do everything you can. And then you accept the fact that the child has limits, and you live with that—and you love the child no less.

You can always change your mind again if circumstances demonstrate that there's new hope, you know. And because you are a grandmother, having to admit that you were wrong when you gave up earlier won't bother you one bit.

🦋 "When Your Cousin Tracy Had This Problem . . ."

As you go through the decades that turn you into a grandmother, you'll have the chance to observe many people as they encounter problems, struggle to solve them, and come out the other side a success or failure or somewhere in between. Most of the time these episodes won't be very exciting (and you'll be glad of that!). But it's wise to store them in your memory all the same, so that when the same problem comes around again, as it probably will, you can bring up the previous occasion as a useful example.

Don't be concerned if the reaction to your advice that starts with, "You know, I remember when your Aunt Elaine had exactly the same problem you're dealing with now," is a sulky, "What do I care what stupid old Elaine did?" or worse. Don't be concerned even if the response to your opening sentence is, "Grandmother, I don't want to *hear* what Aunt Elaine did! Who cares? I'm *not* Aunt Elaine!" This is a natural response. It doesn't mean that what you want to say is really unwelcome.

When you've already presented your example and gotten a negative reaction, say, "Well then, dear, you can ignore what Elaine did and do something else"—and change the subject. You've accomplished your goal of inserting Elaine's solution into the set of possibilities under consideration. You've demonstrated that this problem has happened to other people before and that they've managed to deal with it and get on with their lives. All that you'll do if you try to demand a positive response is make your listener's determination to reject it even stronger, regardless of the consequences.

When you're stopped by a negative reaction before you can even begin talking, don't try to force it. Just say, "I hear you, dear. And that's fine. If you decide later on that you'd like to know how Aunt Elaine handled it, just let me know." Most of the time that will get you a

grudging, "Oh, all right! I know it won't help, but if you really want to tell me about it, Grandmother, I guess it won't kill me to listen." And then you can proceed.

You may be thinking that you should be able to expect more courtesy, something more in the Gracious Living line, when you're doing your best to help. Miss Manners would say so, you're thinking; Martha Stewart would say so. You're quite right, too. If this were a perfect world, the very fact that you love the grandchild and want to help would guarantee that you'd always get a charming and affectionate response. But by the time you become a grandmother you will be well aware that this is *not* a perfect world. It contains sulky and ungrateful and ungracious people galore, and some of them are sure to turn up among your relatives. You can't change that, but you can make the best of it.

And as you do, you are teaching in the most powerful way there is: by example. You are demonstrating the magnificent art of *successful* human communication to your grandchildren. You are modeling that process for them and letting them join in it with you. This way, they can become adults for whom it is second nature because they had the privilege of exposure to it while they were still young enough to learn it with ease and pleasure.

🌺 When You're Part of the Problem

There will be times when you—the grandmother—are the one who is unwilling or uncooperative or unreasonable. You're human; it will happen. And you have no grandmother to turn to. Then what do you do?

You *pretend*, that's what! Sit in front of a mirror, if necessary, and say to yourself all the wise things that you'd say to somebody else in the same circumstances, and then follow your own good advice.

For example, suppose you really dislike the young woman your son chose to marry, or the young man your daughter chose for a husband.

"My grandmother's stationery is so thick it costs her two bucks to mail a letter."

Unanswered Mail

What do you do if you write letters to your grandchildren and they never write you back? You go right on writing to them, and you *don't* include any of the following sentences in your letters:

❖ "If you want Grandmother to keep writing to you, you have to write to her, too."
❖ "Why don't you ever answer my letters? Don't you think you ought to write to me, since I write to you?"
❖ "I love you so much that even if you never write to me I'll still go on writing to you—but it makes me very sad."

That is, no nagging and no guilt tripping! This isn't being a Martyr, it's setting a good example. The fact that a child is not behaving like an adult is no excuse for the adult to behave like a child.

Suppose just the *sight* of this spouse puts your teeth on edge. Then you must sit yourself down and give yourself exactly the same firm counsel that you'd give a grandchild who disliked his or her cousin or sibling. Your responsibility to the family as a role model is far more important than your personal tastes, and you simply have to set those tastes aside. Otherwise, you'll be modeling, for your own grandchildren, what they should *not* do.

You are the grandmother. Rise to the occasion!

❧ If You're a "Long-Distance" Grandmother

There's nothing like being right there when something happens, so you know exactly what's going on. If you don't live near your grandchildren, you won't have that luxury. But that doesn't mean that you can't help, if you're sure that you have enough information to do so.

Tapes and letters have advantages that on-the-spot communication lacks. People can hear or read them in private, where their reactions to what is said won't be an embarrassment to them or make them feel defensive. They can go over your words as many times as they want to, to be sure they've understood. And they can prepare their response to what you've told them far more carefully and thoroughly than is possible when they're face to face with you and are trying to think on their feet.

Chapter 3

◨

Emotional Work

🐛 Thinking Like a Grandmother

··

GRANDMOTHER PRINCIPLE 8:
GRANDMOTHERS DON'T *HAVE* TO BE
POLITICALLY CORRECT.

··

And that's a very good thing! Because the next Grandmother Principle I have to take up in this book is so politically beyond the pale that only a grandmother would *dare* present it.

··

GRANDMOTHER PRINCIPLE 9:
WHEN GETTING SOMEBODY ELSE TO DO A TASK
IS MORE WORK THAN JUST DOING IT YOURSELF,
DO IT YOURSELF.

··

Any parent can clean a child's bedroom in a tenth of the time it takes to get the child to do it, you know. Any parent can do *all* the housework in a tenth of the time it takes to get children to do their "fair share." Deciding exactly what "your fair share of the housework" means can take longer than the tasks involved would take. But parents who

X-Rated Alphabet Soup

always say, "Oh, never mind, I'll do it myself!" will send spoiled and useless adults out into the world one day; it's not a good idea.

Grandmothers aren't responsible for teaching children those lessons, however, and are free to decide when Grandmother Principle 9 can and should be applied. And one area of life where it applies almost without exception is that of *emotional work*.

❧ What Emotional Work Is, Why It Has to Be Done, and Why Grandmothers Should Do It

In *Becoming a Grandmother* Sheila Kitzinger tells us that women are a family's "kin-keepers." I like that word very much. It goes a long way toward explaining what emotional work is and why it's so important. Emotional work is the work that keeps people within a family kin to one another and sustains and nourishes their kinship. It's the work that makes kinship more than a set of cold, dull facts in government documents. And kinship matters desperately if the social fabric is to remain whole. Among the Navajo who are my friends, one of the worst things you can say about others is that they behave as if they had no relatives—no kinfolk. A large part of the job of preventing people from behaving like the kinless is carried out through emotional work.

That being the case, this is work that ought to be highly valued and highly paid; those who do it ought to get our strongest praise and support. Unfortunately, the tasks involved tend to be the sort of things that cause people (especially male people and quite young people of both genders) to say, "Why on earth do you bother doing that?" and "I can't believe you're going to waste your time doing that!" and "Look, there are important things that need doing if you've got all that spare time to waste!"

The list that follows is an assortment of typical emotional-work chores, in no particular order. Some of them have already been discussed in this book; some will be taken up in later chapters.

❖ Addressing and mailing holiday cards.
❖ Sending birthday cards, congratulations cards, get-well cards, and so on, to family members, *even to those who never send a single such card or note themselves.*
❖ Choosing gifts for people, wrapping them, and sending or delivering them—instead of just mailing a check.
❖ Putting family photos in an album, with clear notes to identify the people, places, occasions, and dates.
❖ Remembering and maintaining the family history.
❖ Acting as mediator between quarreling relatives, especially when the quarrel is ridiculous and everybody knows it.
❖ Remembering to praise the child who is too old to be cute and too young to be clever and accomplished, when everyone else is fussing over the babies and congratulating the stars.
❖ Knowing which family members should have something nonalco-

holic in their drink glasses and seeing that it's done without anybody noticing.

* Knowing what sizes everybody wears, and what colors they like and dislike.
* Paying attention to the relatives nobody can stand and carrying on conversations with them anyway—including the ones that you can't stand, either.
* Keeping in touch with distant relatives, especially the elderly ones and the lonely ones.
* Knowing which child collects what, and adding to those collections regularly, even if the collection is something like dead bugs.
* Making gifts with your own two hands instead of buying things.
* Hosting family dinners and reunions and gatherings.
* Finding out, one little scrap at a time, the real reason why a family member has done or is doing some dreadful thing.
* Remembering the family symbols that are important to the little kids, no matter how silly they seem to everyone else.
* Honoring truly stupid ideas that family members get in their heads, as long as they're not dangerous to anyone.

In most families women do these things—all of which are critically important to kin-keeping—along with scores of other similar tasks. Even when they don't do them personally, women are responsible for making sure that they get done. It's not fair, and it's politically outrageous

A Special Gift

Buy a very nice engagement calendar or diary and keep it for a whole year—writing just a few lines a day is enough—and then give it as a gift. If it's a gift for Christmas (or any other occasion that creates a deadline), keep writing in it right up until it's time to wrap it. I've done one of these for each of my grandchildren over the years; I'd give a fortune to have one from either of my own grandmothers.

to acknowledge it, but it's the truth, and nothing useful will be accomplished by pretending otherwise. Let's just get the truth right out here in the open for all to see: *Men don't do these things.* Men can't be bothered, usually, and on the rare occasions when they do bother they expect a medal for their efforts. Men who haven't sent a gift for a decade will be outraged if, when they do send one, they don't get an immediate thank-you note. Getting most men to do this kind of work is far more work than doing it yourself, and will leave you furious, disgusted, and prepared to behave like somebody who has no relatives.

I'm often asked why most men in our culture can't be persuaded to share in the emotional work. I don't know the answer to that question. The fact that cultures exist where men are as likely to do it as women are means it can't be an innate biological characteristic linked with sexual gender. I consider this one of the great unsolved mysteries; I deplore it the way I deplore the fact that human beings aren't able to fly under their own power. I congratulate all those fine men who are the exceptions to the rule. And I encourage scientists to go right ahead and apply for research grants to investigate the phenomenon. As for me, I've said all I can say about it and I intend to move on.

"Women do it" isn't quite narrow enough, however. Grandmothers should be prepared to carry the heaviest share of this load, for four excellent reasons.

1. Grandmothers are better qualified for emotional work than other women in the family. They may not have any more free time than anyone else, overall, but they aren't ordinarily tied to a frantic and rigid schedule the way mothers (and many young women not yet mothers) are. They have far more freedom in the *scheduling* of their time.

2. Grandmothers know more about family matters than the younger women do, simply because they've been around longer and have more experience with it all.

3. Grandmothers have more patience and are less likely to go to pieces or take hasty actions without thinking. Not because they necessarily have more wisdom, but because their vantage point within the family makes them better able to perceive it as a whole.

4. Finally, emotional work takes lots of time and energy and organization, but much of it requires little physical strength. It can be done competently even by someone who is bedridden or housebound or simply frail.

None of this means that grandmothers shouldn't expect the rest of the women in the family to help with the emotional work. On the contrary. The other women need to begin doing these tasks a little at a time, so that when they're grandmothers they'll be adept at them. They have to learn. Furthermore, they need time to work out their own ways of doing things. But the primary responsibility should rest with the grandmothers, whose constant example as kin-keepers is one of the most important parts of grandmothering. And the way that it's done requires careful and constant attention. You *do* want to set the sort of example that makes you indispensable no matter how frail you become and demonstrates vividly how valuable an elderly person is to the family and society. You *don't* want to set the sort of example that makes people say, "Why do I hate Christmas? Because Grandmother drove everybody nuts about it, starting about the first week of February, that's why!"

In later chapters we'll be taking up some of the more long-term emotional-work tasks, such as maintaining the family history and the

Failing Memory

Don't depend on your memory! Get a good organizer system and write things down, so that the only thing you ever have to remember is to look in your organizer at least twice daily. I use a DayTimer™ myself, but there are many others to choose from, including a basic three-ring binder and plenty of notebook paper. You have better things to do with your time and energy than struggle to remember what you could far more easily look up.

family myths and stories. Right now we're going to focus on more immediate tasks.

🦋 Mediating Family Disagreements and Misunderstandings

The majority of family arguments aren't over issues like war and the death penalty and the future of humankind. Most aren't even over issues of grave importance within the family itself, such as whether a couple should move to Oklahoma, whether a son should have to go into a family business, or whether a child's lifestyle should be grounds for

D. Barstow

forbidding that child to enter the house. Most family arguments are of just three kinds:

- ❖ Arguments about money.
- ❖ Arguments about who should do what work.
- ❖ Arguments about trivia.

Grandmothers know this. They are aware that the hour-long wrangles over whether it's okay to feed a baby a bite of bacon at Sunday morning breakfast, whether thirteen is too young for lipstick, and whether the couch should be against the wall or in front of the fire-place—passionate though they all may become—are trivial. If you are a new grandmother you may not yet realize this, but it would dawn on you as the years go by; it will help to find it out right now instead of having to wait for that dawning. And you will become aware that not only are most family arguments over trivia, most of them aren't even over what appears to be the subject of the argument. Grandmother Principle 10 says it all:

GRANDMOTHER PRINCIPLE 10:
MOST ARGUMENTS ARE ABOUT WHO IS IN CHARGE.

Knowing this is critically important, and will make many otherwise mysterious phenomena understandable; the only thing *more* important is keeping that knowledge to yourself. Because otherwise you will have a lot of trouble applying Grandmother Principle 11:

GRANDMOTHER PRINCIPLE 11:
IT'S ALWAYS *SAFE* TO TALK TO A GRANDMOTHER.

The seven basic rules of grandmotherly mediation that follow from GP10 and GP11 are easily stated and remembered, although they may run contrary to your natural inclinations.

1. Never say that an argument is trivial; to the people involved, it probably seemed important at the time. If one of them tells you later that it's not important, never say, "Oh, I knew that all along!" Say, "I'm glad to know that and I thank you for telling me."

2. Unless it's absolutely impossible to arrange, do your mediation with each arguing person individually and in private. And never betray the confidences that are given to you in those private sessions. Ask for permission. Say, "Anna, would you be willing to let me tell William that you don't really think of him as a cheap crook?" If the answer is no, keep Anna's secret. But say, "I know you won't want to let William go on believing you despise him when that's not true; you're not that sort of person. When you're ready for me to tell him, you just let me know." And then add, "Of course, you may decide you'd rather tell him yourself."

3. Don't try mediation until the people involved have had a chance to calm down a little. The Bible tells us not to let the sun go down on our anger, and that, like being perfect, is a worthy goal to strive toward. While the striving goes on, however, remember this: it's a heck of a lot better for anger and bad feeling to go on for two weeks than for it to go on for *years*. If you have to wait a few days before the opponents in the argument are willing to discuss it with you, let that time go by. What matters is that peace be made, not that it be made instantly.

4. When mediating, *listen*. Let the angry person talk it all out, without interrupting or contradicting, and listen with your full attention until it's over. Otherwise, what *you* have to say will go in one ear and out the other.

5. Try not to diagnose, preach, or psychoanalyze; try not to offer unasked-for advice. Usually the angry person will ask you questions like, "What do you think I should do?" and "Do you think I overreacted?" in which case it's okay to answer, briefly. If that doesn't happen and you feel that you need to express your opinion anyway, say, "Would you be willing to let me tell you what I think went

wrong?" (This is a way of saying, "You are in charge," which is, you will remember, what it's all about.) If the answer is no, say, "Fine, it's up to you."

6. Don't waste your time. If the angry person is stubborn, vindictive, uncooperative, and interested only in showing off all these qualities for you, let it pass. Make a note somewhere: "Saturday afternoon, May 3: Marvin in stupid argument with Kim over how much rain fell last April, then in stupid argument with me over why the argument wasn't really stupid. Waste of time. Try again in about six weeks."

7. Always be willing to give an angry person another chance. That is, suppose that two years later Marvin comes to you and says, "Grandmother, do you think maybe you could talk to Kim and tell her I'm sorry I fought with her over how much it rained? And find out if she's willing to speak to me again now that I've come to my senses?" Just say you'd be glad to do it—and nothing more—and get on with it.

These seven rules, combined with the Grandmother Principles and your own reliable common sense, will carry you through most family disagreements and misunderstandings.

🦋 Comforting Losers

Losing an argument can be very painful, no matter how tiny and piddling the issue. When the loser is ready to admit that, offering comfort is easy. You just say, "That was awful for you; I'm so glad it's over." And when the loser says, "I'll never, never be able to forget it, as long as I live! I'll never be able to talk to him [or her] again, ever!" don't argue. Say, "I hear you." Say, "People have a hard time forgetting words that hurt and arguments that go wrong." Say, "Life isn't easy." Say, "Families can be a real drag." If nothing else comes to mind, say, "Honey, nobody can tell which way the train went by looking at the tracks." The message you're trying to convey isn't an analysis of the argument or a critique of the characters of the people involved, it's "I love you anyway, and I have faith in you."

🦋 Bringing Winners Down Gently a Peg or Two

Many arguments are won by brute force. One person manages to yell louder than anybody else or cry more hysterically than anybody else or simply outlast everybody else. When such a victory leaves the winner shaken and stunned and sorry, that's fine; that's how it ought to be. But the winner who struts around the place afterward, thrilled with his or her own importance and power needs a quick trim from you—in private.

Suppose Marvin wins, and when he's alone with you he says, "Boy, I guess I told *her*, didn't I? I guess she'll think twice before she takes *me* on again! " Smile. Say, "You're quite right. Yes indeed. A few more sessions like that, dear, and you'll be able to spend all your holidays entirely alone, just like you planned on doing." And then listen to the outburst, and when it's over say how glad you are to learn that you misunderstood his intentions, followed by, "You'll have to excuse me now, dear; I've got envelopes to address."

🦋 Transmitting Negative Messages Without Causing Anybody Involved to Lose Face

There is a widely held belief that negative message content must be given a negative shape. That's not true, thank goodness. Suppose you need to tell your granddaughter Tammy that the version of a family story she has just used to win an argument is totally inaccurate, which will mean that she has to apologize and take it all back. You *could* say this: "Really, Tammy, you'd think you'd have brains enough to get your FACTS straight before you start SPOUTING them! Your Great-Aunt Carla not only did NOT say you're supposed to inherit the grand piano, it wasn't even HERS! HONESTLY!"

You could say that, yes; I've heard a lot of talk of that kind in my time. But consider Tammy's situation. She'll have to go to the siblings she argued with about that piano and admit that she was wrong, admit that the piano won't necessarily be hers—and might turn out to be theirs!—and apologize for the things she said, all at the same time. This is the kind of exchange that can leave family members refusing to speak to one another for years. The loss of face for Tammy is going to be enormous, unless she has saintly siblings. For you to make that loss of face even worse with a lambasting like the example above would be justifiable only if no other way of getting the message across existed. That's not the case; while she's talking to *you*, you can leave her her dignity.

The first thing that could be done to make that chunk of language less hostile would be to get all the extra emphasis out of it. To hear what I mean, read it aloud and bear down hard on all the words that are written in capital letters. Hear that tune? *That is the melody of English-language hostility.* If you take all that out and set the same words to a neutral tune, it will help a little. It's important, when speaking any negative message, to make sure you don't add the spoken equivalent of all those capital letters. But it would be even better to talk to Tammy—in private—like this:

You: Tammy, I have something to tell you that isn't going to be easy to hear. Are you ready for it?

Tammy: I guess so.

You: Honey, that grand piano didn't belong to your Great-Aunt Carla. It was Uncle Frank's piano. He won it in a sweepstakes when he was nineteen years old.

Tammy: But Aunt Carla *said* she was leaving it to *me!*

You: People sometimes say things they have no right to say; it happens.

Tammy: Oh, no! This is horrible!

You: It sure is. It's not going to be easy for you to set this right; I know that. But I know you can do it.

For you to argue with Tammy about whether Great-Aunt Carla did or didn't say she could have the piano, even if you're positive Carla never said any such thing, is buying into the idea that the point of arguing is to *win* so that you can prove that you're in charge. It's irrelevant; it makes no difference at all. Let it go.

Now suppose Tammy says no, she isn't ready to hear your bad news. Suppose she says, "No! WHATEVER it is, I don't want to HEAR it!" Then what? Then you say, "I'm sorry you feel that way. I'm always sorry to have to tell somebody bad news they'd rather not hear. If I had a choice, I wouldn't do it this time, either. I don't have a choice." And then, "Honey, that grand piano didn't belong to your Great-Aunt Carla. . . ." And so on.

I Know I Shouldn't Say This, But . . .

One of the most irritating of all language patterns in English is the *Hedge*, which lets you take back what you say before you say it, and then go ahead and say it all the same. As in "I know this is a stupid question, but . . ." followed by the question you know is stupid. The natural reaction to such sequences is resentment and an unspoken "If you know you shouldn't say it, why *do* you say it?" Never use a Hedge if you can avoid it; clip every one that comes to your mind, if possible. Like this:

❖ Don't say: "I know this is a stupid question, but I have to ask it. Are we lost?"

❖ Say: "I know this is a stupid question. I'm sorry I have to ask it. Are we lost?"

❖ Don't say: "I know you're not going to like it if I tell you what to do, but you really should stop and ask for directions."

❖ Say: "I know you're not going to like it if I tell you what to do. Nobody does—and they're quite right. I really believe you should stop and ask for directions."

It's your responsibility to straighten out messes of this kind by providing accurate information. But you don't have to do it with hostile language that adds insult to injury. Use your Velvet Glove.

Making someone lose face is almost always a mistake. In our society it has two inevitable consequences, and both are destructive to the family. First, people who've lost face will go looking for someone weaker to pick on, to make themselves feel competent again; you're just passing the meanness along, like salmonella. Second, people who've lost face will hold a grudge about it and hunker down to wait for chances to get revenge. You don't need that, and your family doesn't need that. The brief feeling of satisfaction that comes from causing well-deserved loss of face isn't worth the trouble it guarantees down the road. The only way grandmothers can be successful mediators is by steadfastly maintaining their status as people that even the most unpleasant family members feel safe talking to. For the sake of the rest of the family, you need to safeguard that status. You may well be the *only* person some unpleasant relative feels safe talking to frankly and openly, and that can be critically important in family struggles and disputes.

🦋 Making Hard Decisions No One Else Is Willing to Make

In every family there are times when it's clear that something unwelcome has to be done. The family farm has to be sold. The family business has to be shut down. An elderly relative has to be moved to a nursing home for his or her own safety. A grandchild has been counting on a promised trip to Europe before college, but the money for such a trip just isn't there and the trip has to be forgotten. Unwelcome decisions range from the genuinely trivial ("No, honey, you cannot have a $500 collector's edition Star Trek night-light") to those that tear people's lives apart, and even the trivial ones seem momentous to someone whose heart is set on them.

One of the most useful things grandmothers can do—once all the alternatives have been explored and it's certain that no other choice but the unwelcome one remains, and once it's obvious that nobody else is willing or able to take responsibility—is to step in and be the Designated Decision Announcer. You don't want to do this too soon. You want to wait until all the conditions have been met and no question remains. But when that time arrives, you will do everyone a valuable service by saying, straight out, what nobody else can bring themselves to say: "Well, in *my* opinion, we have to sell the farm. It's too bad, but it has to be done." This will let the rest of the family stop sitting around wringing their hands and get started with the dreadful task, whatever it may be.

And what if you make a mistake? It's a horrible thought, but it's certainly possible. What if, later, you learn that another option did exist, but "since Grandmother really had her heart set on it" they reluctantly did what you said?

Hold this thought: You are a grandmother, not a wizard! You can't know everything; you can't foresee the future; you can't always be right. Don't torment yourself about it. Someone in the family has to be willing to make hard decisions, even if they turn out to be wrong. As long as everyone else has had a chance to state their preferences and objections and get a fair hearing, and no one had the courage to step forward and take responsibility, the error is as much their fault as yours. Put it behind you and move on to the next quandary.

🦋 Taking the Heat Without Getting Burned

Grandmothers can usefully take the heat for many things; they are in many ways heatproof. They can't be fired or demoted or lose tenure; like Supreme Court justices, they are secure in their slots for life. If the children and grandchildren want to claim that the reason they vacation in Ohio instead of Hawaii is because they're catering to your desires, and you know that the real reason is that they can't afford Hawaii or are afraid to fly, let it pass. Nothing will be gained by forcing them to admit that they're using you as an excuse.

On the other hand, you don't have to allow this kind of thing to be carried to ridiculous extremes. If that appears to be likely, arrange to meet the relative at the heart of the strategy and state your case, in the most neutral possible fashion. Like this: "Jeffrey, I know I can count on you to realize that there are limits to the amount of heat I'm willing to take. I know I can count on you not to abuse the privilege of blaming decisions on me. I'm confident that in the future you will always check with me to be sure it's okay to say something is happening only because that's what Grandmother wants. It makes me very proud to know that I don't have to worry about any of these things, because you are a trustworthy and sensible person."

Jeffrey has now been warned, courteously and gently. And if it doesn't work, the first time you find yourself being used as an excuse without permission, speak right up and set the record straight. Like this: "You know, Jeffrey has been so busy that he's lost track of one important fact: that I really don't mind at all if you kids go to Disneyland for the Fourth of July."

𝕯 Taking Over—Temporarily—When It Can't be Avoided, and Abdicating Instantly When the Crisis Is Past

We read sad tales these days about grandmothers who are serving as full-time mothers for their grandchildren because the kids' parents are off somewhere "following their bliss" or for even more tragic reasons. If this is your situation, you have my heartfelt sympathy. It must be awful. I don't know how on earth I would manage if it happened to me. In such cases, you have to rely on your parenting skills, not the grandparenting ones.

But suppose, as is usually the case, that the crisis suddenly putting you on full alert is temporary. That's different. The most typical crisis calling for extraordinary effort from you is when a parent is suddenly taken ill or injured, and someone is needed to take over the household. When this happens, you have to make a hard decision. Unless you are literally incapable of doing so, you *should* take over in a twenty-four-hour crisis. However difficult and inconvenient and complicated that may be, everyone involved can muddle through for that period of time and survive the experience without significant damage. Beyond twenty-four hours, however, you have to stop and ask yourself, "Am I willing to do this? And am I able to?" and you have to answer honestly. Let's wade right into this and get it settled, because it is not the case that grandmothers *must* take over when asked. Let me give you an example.

I have a neurological glitch that makes my balance very poor at all times and causes sudden episodes of severe vertigo with no warning whatsoever. For me to have taken over the households of any of my children, when that would have meant that I personally had to carry a tiny child, would have put that child in danger. I knew that, and I didn't risk it. Refusing wasn't easy, because after decades of coping with my balance problems I've learned to manage pretty well. When a beloved child was asking for my help, the temptation to say, "Of course I'll come look after things!" was strong. The pressure to do it was also strong. Children in desperate straits are human, and they do say things like, "Oh, Mother, you haven't fallen down for *ages!*" They may believe what they're saying; if you aren't a chronic complainer, they probably *do* believe it, and they may therefore hold your refusal against you. Nevertheless, I knew that until they could walk my grandchildren were safer with strangers than with me, and I stuck to my guns. And I was right to do so.

If you're not physically and/or emotionally able to look after a household, don't try—and if you don't want your reasons known, don't state them. Just say, "I'm sorry, children; I have to say no," and let whatever is said in response go right on by. With the privilege of not stating your reasons comes the responsibility of accepting the resulting bad feeling; that's just the way it is. Finally, if you're capable of doing the job, but you know that you'll end up hating both your grandchildren and their parents if you say yes, you should still say no. If you weren't around,

Grandparents Raising Grandchildren

❖ A booklet with basic information for grandparents facing this difficult situation is available for $3.00 (to cover postage and handling) from The National Foster Parent Association, 9 Dartmoor Drive, Crystal Lake IL 60014 (815-455-2527); ask for "Grandparents Raising Grandchildren: A Guide to Finding Help and Hope."

❖ A free fact sheet for caregiver grandprents is available from Katrina W. Johnson, Attention: Grandparents: Facts That You May Not Know, Behavioral and Social Research Program, National Institute on Aging, Gateway Building, Suite 533, Bethesda MD 20892.

❖ There's an Internet support group for grandparents who are the primary caregivers for their grandchildren. You can join by sending an e-mail message with subject line blank to: majordomo@majordomo.pobox.com. For the message, type in just two words: subscribe grandparents. Susan Miles (a grandmother raising three preschool grandkids) runs this list; if you have questions, you can reach her at: susan.miles@cmich.edu. The list will introduce you to many other sources, such as the "Grandparents Parenting . . . Again" and "GrandsRuS—Grandparents Raising Grandchildren" Web sites.

your family would have to make other arrangements; they'll manage. If your financial circumstances make it possible for you to help with those other arrangements, by all means do that; if not, it can't be helped. Think it over carefully, make an honest decision, and stick to it. Because playing the Martyr role, although it may seem like the easiest choice at the time, will create bad feeling of a far uglier and more dangerous kind than will refusing to help.

Instant Housecleaning

There will be occasions when you don't have time to get the house clean, but it's important for it to *look* as if you keep it meticulously—for example, when someone calls with no prior warning and says, "We'll be there in twenty minutes!" Here's what you do:

* Make the beds.
* Wash the dishes, if you have time—if not, put them in a sink full of hot soapy water or in the dishwasher.
* Close the doors to all the rooms except the living room and kitchen.
* Put all the clutter in a closet and close the door.
* Put all the dirty laundry in the washer.

Whenever you have *no* time to clean—say you're tending four small grandkids with food poisoning—put the vacuum cleaner in the middle of the living room floor and leave it there, plugged in. The message to anyone who drops in is that they've interrupted you right in the middle of a major cleaning effort.

"I'll be the first to admit, sometimes I just sweep the dust under the carpet."

You may be wondering why this section is in the chapter on emotional work. *It's because that's where it belongs.* The truth is, for the majority of grandmothers the real difficulty with taking over a household isn't the physical work. Most grandmothers have already raised at least one child; they've already kept a house for years and years; they know how. In minutes they can breeze through physical tasks that take young parents hours to do. I can get all the urgent housework done in an average house before nine o'clock in the morning, including putting that night's dinner together, and not even be breathing fast—even with three or four small kids running around while I do it. This isn't because I'm a superb homemaker; I most emphatically am not. It's because I've done it all so long that I could do it in my sleep. The hard part, for most grandmothers, is always going to be the emotional work. For example . . .

While you're running the household, you should run it just as well as it *must* be run, and not one scrap better than that. Use paper plates and plastic cutlery. Make peanut butter sandwiches. Let a little dust collect in places where it does no harm. It won't be helpful to your chadults, after you leave, to have the grandchildren sayings things like, "Well, when Grandmother was taking care of us, she always made pancakes for breakfast, and she *never* gave us icky cold cereal like *you* do!" *Aim for the middle ground.*

You don't want your grandchildren to do without anything they really need. You don't want them living in squalor. But you also don't want to set standards that their parents won't be able to live up to after you leave, or standards that make them look inadequate by comparison with you. When the grandchildren are visiting at *your* house, you can do what you like, including spotlessness everywhere and stuffed nightingales three times daily, if that's your style. But when you're looking after them at *their* house—or have taken them home to your place only for the duration of an emergency—you have an obligation to protect not only their health and welfare but also the image they have of their parents.

If you find the household that you're rescuing is in a mess, by your standards, *you should leave it that way.* I don't mean that if you take over

"Mom, tell me again about the blue ribbons Grandma won at the State Fair for her silky devil's food cake."

after a household has gone downhill during someone's grave illness or crisis you shouldn't pitch in and set it right—not at all. I mean that if your chadults pile up their towels in the linen closet any old way, instead of folding them neatly and stacking them by colors and patterns as you do, you should follow their system and pile up their towels any old way while you're there. It's even more important to remember this when the household is one where you feel a genuine dislike for one of its adults—for your child's spouse, for example. The temptation to show the person toward whom you harbor negative feelings "a thing or two" can be sneaky and overwhelming. Resist it with all your might.

None of this is easy. Your natural tendency will be to aim for the extremes—either by doing as little as is humanly possible because you resent having to do it at all and want to make sure that will be understood by everyone involved, or by doing a superb job to demonstrate to your grandchildren how a *real* expert runs a home. Both of those natural

Icing Cakes

If you enjoy fussing with icing, by all means go right ahead. If you don't, here are two ways to avoid it, both preapproved by my own grandchildren in controlled experiments:

1. Wait until the last minute, and then spread a whole tub or can of "whipped topping" over the top of the cake. (It will start melting after a while in warm air.)
2. Put a cup of confectioner's sugar or powdered sugar in the bottom of a small bowl. Add unsweetened lemon juice, a little bit at a time, stirring as you go, until you have something just barely liquid enough to pour. (If you go too far with the lemon juice, no problem; just add some more sugar.) Pour it over your cake and let it run down the sides. This is especially good on chocolate cakes.

Two Treats My Grandmother Lewis Taught Me

These two treats—which can be made at lightning speed—are guaranteed to delight small children, even those whose palates have been ruined with junk food.

❖ **Piecrust cookies:** Make a piecrust using any recipe you're happy with. Roll it out (it makes no difference what shape it takes). Sprinkle it with sugar and cinnamon. Put it on a baking sheet, and then—gently—cut it into squares or slices. Bake at about 375°F (190°C) until lightly browned.
❖ **Toasted crackers:** Butter some ordinary saltines. Put them on a baking sheet. Bake at 400°F (205°C) just until the butter melts and the tops turn light brown—roughly three minutes, depending on your oven.

tendencies should be resisted with vigor, and that resistance is a lot more work than the household tasks are.

In addition, you need to follow Grandmother Principle 12, which is short and sweet:

··

GRANDMOTHER PRINCIPLE 12:
GRANDMOTHERS *DELEGATE*.

··

Your grandchildren are going to be worried about the absent parent or parents, worried about how long their lives will be turned upside down, worried about how you're going to do things, and worried about all the hundreds of items they worry about even in routine circumstances. If only one parent is absent, the other parent will have all those worries to deal with, too—plus the burden of guilt because he or she couldn't manage without calling on you for help. The best thing you can do for all these worried people is give them as much of the household labor to do as they can handle. And not just to keep them busy, so that they don't have as much time to brood. That's important, and it's common sense, but it's not all. You also do this so that when the crisis is over they'll be able to say truthfully that they were a vital part of the Crisis Crew while it lasted. So that in later years there'll be a family story along the lines of, "Remember the time Mama was in the hospital for so long and Grandma came and stayed with us and I fixed breakfast every single day, all by myself?"

This is a special case. Grandmother Principle 9 says that when getting others to do things is more trouble than doing it yourself you should feel free to do it yourself. But in this special circumstance, it's okay to ask a small grandchild to set the table, even if it takes the child half an hour to do it. It's okay to have a grandchild serve cold cereal for breakfast every day, even if it gets boring and offends your sensibilities. It's okay to have the children's father clean the bathtub, even if he leaves a ring of cleanser where the ring of dirt was before he cleaned.

What's *not* okay is delegating a task and then butting in and managing the way it's done. Only in emergencies—when a grandchild is just about to take the toast out of the plugged-in toaster with a fork—do you step in, as unobtrusively as you can manage.

It's also not okay (except in emergencies) to delegate a task and then complain about how it was done, or do it over yourself afterwards. My French mother-in-law, when her son and I were living with her, would come into our bedroom in the wee hours of the morning, take away the shirts I'd spent hours ironing that day, re-iron them (*magnificently*, needless to say) and then put them away again in the dresser drawers. I assume she believed that she was so silent that I never heard her come and go, and that I was so stupid that I couldn't tell the difference between her perfect ironing and the mess I always made of it. (This was before the days of permanent press, and the French shirts were heavy cotton and heavy linen, double-cuffed, horrible to iron.) I'm certain that she meant well. She was determined to spare her son and the rest of us the public embarrassment of wrinkled shirts. But I was *so* ashamed! It was a bitter and constant humiliation until I finally learned to iron well enough to meet French standards. Grandmothers will spare themselves a lot of work and lost sleep, and their family members a lot of misery, by refraining from that kind of thing.

As soon as the crisis is over—never mind how many half-done tasks there are—you must hand the household back to its rightful keepers and *leave*, for your own sake and for everyone else's. Don't linger. Don't hover. You will probably have discovered things during your stay—things about the way your chadults ordinarily run the place, like the pitiful way I ironed my husband's shirts—that will make you feel that you'd be abandoning the family by leaving. Never mind that either. Stay as long as people truly cannot manage without you. Leave the instant that's no longer true.

❧ Maintaining Your Image

The only part of your image that requires maintenance where emotional work is concerned is the image of consistency and reliability.

"But can your grandma sing and brush her teeth at the same time?"

The point is not that you should produce holiday cards in exquisite taste, addressed and signed in an elegant hand. If you do, if it comes naturally to you, good for you. But that's not what matters. What matters is that your grandchildren will be able to say fondly that you *always* sent a card, every single year, until you were too superannuated to hold a pen or hit a key, whichever happens to be your preferred way of doing it.

The point is not that you should host family dinners of gourmet quality, in a home so flawlessly kept that it appears to be on exhibit or for sale. The point is not that the conversations you preside over on such occasions should be of salon quality, with never a hint of the disagreeable or the ordinary. The point is that your grandchildren, when they come upon hard and lonely times in later life, should have an ample store of memories of family gatherings with you at which they felt safe and comfortable and loved.

The point is not that you should do all (or any) of these things perfectly, but that you should always appear to be doing them easily, lovingly, and—above all—with pleasure.

If You're a "Long-Distance" Grandmother

Many of the tasks on the list of emotional work on pages 68–69 are just as easily done at a distance as nearby. Some may even be easier, because you're less likely to be interrupted by grandchildren running in and out of your house and needing your direct attention. But the task of temporarily taking over a household in a crisis can't be done long distance. You will want to help nevertheless. What can you do?

You can of course travel straight to the household in crisis and take over, from wherever in the world you may be. If that's possible for you it's an excellent move, as long as you heed all the warnings that have appeared earlier in this chapter. A "long-distance" Martyr is no improvement on one who lives next door; do it willingly and graciously, or don't do it at all.

If you can't lend a hand in person, what matters most is that you get in touch with those who are helping, whether they are relatives or strangers. Contact them immediately, and say, "I can't be there with you, and I know things are really difficult. Is there anything I can do to help?" Even if the answer turns out to be no, the fact that you offered, right away and without reservation, will matter to those carrying the load, and they will remember. If the answer is yes, do your best to follow through on your offer and carry out whatever task is handed to you; that will be remembered, too.

Chapter 4

◨

Resources— Money, Time, and Energy

R *esources.* In grade school we learned to think of resources as copper and steel and petroleum and water. Those are indeed resources, and as valuable as ever, but we won't be discussing them in this chapter; they are rarely the concern of grandmothers. Information, which is a grandmother's most valuable resource, is the subject of this entire book; we have been discussing its use and management and stewardship, and will continue to do so. In this chapter we will narrow our focus to three other resources that are under your control: your own money, your own time, and your own energy. They interact in complicated ways, and we won't try to keep them artificially separated. We'll discuss them all together.

✤ Thinking Like a Grandmother

N othing is more grandmotherly than thinking of money in terms of the way it grows with time—the phenomenon known everywhere as "the miracle of compound interest." Janet Bodnar's *Kiplinger's Money-Smart Kids* gives us a riveting example of the way this miracle works.

Suppose you'd like your grandchild to have about $1,000,000 at age sixty-five. You can see to that yourself, without being either a

Grandparenting Resources

❖ Write to the Foundation for Grandparenting, 5 Casa del Oro Lane, Santa Fe NM 87505. (You can also reach them by e-mail at: gpfound@trail.com.) They can direct you to a wealth of sources of information.

❖ Contact the Grandparent Information Center run by AARP, at 601 E Street NW, Washington DC 20049; the phone is (202) 434-2296.

❖ Do an Internet search for the word *grandparenting* (and related words such as *grandmother* and *grandfather* and *grandchildren*). Check out the "parenting" sites as well, because many of them have grandparent sections. You'll be amazed at all the useful things available to you at little or no cost. Two sites to start with are Senior Mall (http://www.seniormall.org) and "Dear Joan," an advice column for seniors (http://www.thirdage.com).

Note: Internet addresses change constantly and without warning. If you can't find a site I've mentioned, just use its name for an Internet search; the new address may turn up among the listings.

Kennedy or a Rockefeller. You just put $2,000 and change, at the child's birth, in an investment that will pay a steady 10 percent interest—and make sure that not a penny of it gets spent until the child reaches sixty-five. There are also investment funds that offer specialized accounts for this purpose, such as the Twentieth Century Fund's "Giftrust" accounts. Bodnar writes of a grandmother who opened $250 trust accounts in that fund for her seven grandchildren in 1970; by the time the accounts mature in 2015, if they continue to grow as they are growing now, each one will hold roughly $250,000.

Even when you can't start with a full $2,000, even when the investment earns less than 10 percent, even when you allow for normal inflation, a small chunk of money left in an account to grow instead of being spent becomes an astonishingly large chunk of money over time. Most grandmothers can't afford to give their grandchildren large lump sums of money, and probably shouldn't do so even if they're able (see page 105)—but very modest investments, if made early enough in a child's life and left to grow, can make a major difference in a child's adult life. It's much wiser for grandmothers to give this sort of gift to

Gardens

The standard garden—the one with the flawless plants and nary a weed in sight—is needlessly complicated. Its major function is to show off for *people;* the plants aren't impressed. When you plant a garden, put down at least two inches of mulch (more is better). Hay is a good choice, and you can buy it cheaply by the bale. Seeds that would come up easily in bare dirt (like beans) will come up just as easily through the mulch. Seeds that are too frail for that should be started inside anyway and then transplanted when they're big enough—just pull back the mulch, put the seedling into the ground, and tuck the mulch back around it the way you'd tuck covers round a baby.

Mulched gardens fare better. They need less water, and the mulch keeps the plants cooler in hot weather and warmer in cold weather. You don't have to hover over them the way you do with naked gardens. Weeds come up through mulch just like other plants do, but you can pull up mulched weeds with no effort at all; you won't need a hoe. You can wait to pull weeds out of mulch until they're big enough to get a grip on, with no harm done. And the truth is that you can leave most of the weeds, in spite of what you read, and healthy plants won't even notice. Weeds generally don't "compete" with other plants, they cooperate with them.

new babies (and to older children as well) than to put hundreds of dollars into fancy outfits and expensive toys.

There isn't any corresponding "miracle of compound time and energy," unfortunately. But when the well-being of your family is your goal, you can make no better use of time and energy than to spend both with your grandchildren. You have little direct control over the way your grandchildren are cared for and raised. Remember, however, that we now have indisputable evidence that children can do well, even in truly dysfunctional homes, as long as they have one adult they can absolutely count on. Being that adult can mean that your grandchild grows up to be a competent person who is able to function independently and successfully in this world. That outcome is in your own best interest as well as your family's, because such people—real grown-ups—not only are what you naturally want your grandchildren to become but will be

"Grandma says when are we coming to visit? She's starting a new compost heap."

far more useful to you when you are one of the "old old" than weaklings and whiners and wastrels and feckless charmers could ever be.

❧ Staying Solvent Yourself

The goals described above have everything to recommend them, but you have to remember that your resources are finite. Even if you're a multimillionaire grandmother, your personal time and personal

Tips for Traveling with Kids

By the time you're a grandmother you'll know all the "travel tips" information that appears in women's magazines, such as packing a bag of toys and treats and activities for each child, making sure nothing sticky or sharp is in that bag, not letting the child get into the bag until you're under way, insisting that each child get a drink of water and go to the bathroom before leaving, and establishing in advance that as long as you're on the road the child is not allowed to say, "Are we there yet?" or "I'm bored." What you may not realize is that the most important part of traveling with kids is your attitude toward the experience. The right travel-with-kids attitude requires that you accept the following, in advance:

❖ No matter how careful you are, you'll forget something important and be sorry you did.

❖ No matter how many toys and treats and activities you take for the kids, they won't last the whole trip.

❖ Things you're not prepared for will happen, and they may be pretty difficult to deal with; sometimes they will be splendid and wonderful, but don't count on that.

❖ Eventually, the trip will come to an end. Always.

energy will have stern limits. You have to respect those limits. Bankrupting yourself of *any* of your resources in your efforts to be a terrific grandmother is always a serious error. It will leave you helpless to do anything more and is all too likely to mean that your family ends up having to look after *you*.

It's normal for a woman past forty—let alone past sixty—to get tired more quickly than younger people do. I know grandmothers who will agree to take a bunch of kids to the zoo or on some similar expedition for the day, even though they know full well that they'll have to spend the next three days lying down to recover from that outlay of time and energy. Once in a great while, this makes sense. If you are a grandmother who sees your grandkids only once or twice a year, it may make excellent sense. But for most grandmothers it's foolish. It's like spending your entire month's income in one morning, on ice cream. Suppose you agree to one of these overexpenditures and your family suddenly needs your help in even a minor crisis the following day? What will you do then? You can overspend time and energy once or twice, you can force your exhausted self to go on a bit longer now and then, but this sort of extravagance will get you in the end. This is not something to be ashamed of or to worry about; it is the natural course of life. The relevant Grandmother Principle is GP 13:

....

GRANDMOTHER PRINCIPLE 13:
A GRANDMOTHER IS NOT A QUARTERBACK.

....

You aren't in charge of copper and petroleum; you are in charge of your time and energy. *Schedule* them! If you know that one hour of interaction with a boisterous child is all you can manage without suffering for it later, and you have three grandchildren, make it clear that you'll see them one at a time for an hour each, in equal turns. Tell them that if they all want to do something with you at the same time it has to be something that takes only thirty minutes. If you invite them to your house, even with their parents along, put limits on the invitation in advance, and set those limits on the basis of *your* needs. This isn't

To Childproof or Not to Childproof?

All grandmothers whose grandchildren come to visit face this question. There are companies out there selling extraordinarily elaborate arrays of child safety gadgets; you can, if you choose, equip every single object in your house with its own little barriers and locks and keys. I don't think that's wise, and I never did it for either my children or my grandchildren. Children who are treated as if they have no sense at all will oblige you by behaving that way. And come the day they leave the cocoon you've surrounded them with, they'll get hurt because they've learned no survival skills. You don't want infants and toddlers to be in danger in your home; on the other hand, you don't want to send a child off to kindergarten who has never learned not to drink the jug of fingerpaint or jump out the schoolroom windows. There's a middle ground:

* Stairs and windows and balconies must be blocked off securely.
* Dangerous substances—for example, housecleaning products and medicines (including over-the-counter medicines and vitamins and the like)—must either be put out of reach or locked away.
* Guns and knives and matches and cigarette lighters must never be where children can get to them.
* There must be a barrier between the children and anything truly *hot*, and any pan on the stove must have its handle turned toward the back so children can't grab it.
* The hot water must be set at a level that won't scald a child; if that's impossible, there must be a barrier between the child and the faucets.
* Anything children could strangle themselves with—cords

hanging from curtains or shades, for example—must be out of their reach; anything they could choke on must be put away.

❖ Anything with the kind of sharp corners that could injure a stumbling toddler's eyes must either be put away, have its corners temporarily padded, or be blocked off.

Much of the above can be accomplished by four measures. First, make ample use of a safe modern playpen. (When my kids were tiny, I always put the Christmas tree and the presents inside a playpen; I recommend that.) Second, from the time children start to creep, teach them to freeze on command, so that if you see a child taking the top off a bottle of lemon cleanser and you say "Freeze!" that child will hold absolutely still and move nothing, long enough for you either to reach the child or give additional instructions. (You don't have to say the word in a way that's terrifying, just a way that makes it clear that you mean it; my own kids were also taught to freeze when I snapped my fingers at them, so that I only had to say "Freeze" when things were noisy; this saved a lot of embarassment in public places and other people's houses). Third, from Day One, teach children that before they touch things or pick things up or open things they must ask for permission and wait until they have it; if you can't do that, double your other precautions. Fourth: WATCH the children! When your full attention is on a television set, a telephone conversation, a meal being cooked, a salesperson at your door, or any similar distraction, the children belong in a playpen or a crib or under someone else's watchful gaze. Never take it for granted that a child is "too little" to turn over, stand up, creep, and so on—there's always going to be a first time.

selfish, and it isn't being a wimp, it's the way to make sure that your children and grandchildren will look forward to being with you instead of dreading it. You budget your money; as you grow older you have to learn to budget your time and your energy in exactly the same way and for exactly the same good reasons.

I know many families where everyone goes to grandmother's house for gatherings, has a good time for an hour or two, and then sits around miserably waiting for a signal from the grandmother that it's okay to leave. In every case, the grandmother is at least as miserable as they are and is wondering what on earth she might do to get them to go home. And when the end does somehow arrive, finally, both grandmother and relatives say the same thing to themselves once the other is out of earshot: "Thank goodness *that's* over! I thought it would *never* end!" Why this happens in otherwise sane and sensible families I will never know, but it's so common that it even has a technical name; it's called the Abilene Paradox. It means that everyone in a group wants the same thing but nobody gets it because nobody realizes that everybody else wants it. It's absurd.

The easiest way to handle this is to make a calendar at the beginning of every month, put your schedule on it, and send a copy to each family group involved. Clearly indicate on it the times you plan to spend together; write in the hour that you've reserved for each grandchild, any planned baby-sitting, and all planned gatherings. Post your own copy on the front of your refrigerator.

Suppose we're talking about November, with Thanksgiving dinner at your place. The calendar will then have a note on the space for Thanksgiving Day that reads "Thanksgiving at Grandmother's, 11:00 to 3:30." Mailing it out well ahead of time gives people a chance to call you and ask if it's okay to change the time so that a grandchild can get to a church or school function, or whatever the conflict may be. It makes it possible for the schedule to be negotiated until the timing is as right for everyone, including you, as can reasonably be expected. It makes it possible to add and delete items without wreaking havoc. And if some of your family members are overly casual about schedules, the calendar will

help; a week before the event, you call them and say, "I'm checking to be sure you remember that we're celebrating Thanksgiving here next Thursday and I'm expecting you from eleven to about three-thirty. Is that still convenient for you?"

This way, on Thanksgiving Day (or any other occasion your family celebrates together) *everyone* will know that at about three-thirty in the afternoon they can start leaving, without hurting your feelings or anybody else's. And this lets them safely schedule whatever other things they may want to do that day, on either side of the block of hours you've written on the calendar.

This doesn't mean that if everyone, including you, is having a wonderful time at three-thirty you have to stand up and throw them all out that very instant. Three-thirty is a target; it's not set in stone. But you have to stand by the hours you've set, approximately, because you're the one setting an example for the others. They have to be convinced that when you set limits, you *mean* it, or they won't feel free to

"Dear Magic Granny . . ."

Dear Magic Granny,
My daughter's husband just *will not* join the rest of us at family gatherings. He insists on watching television the whole time we're trying to vist, and none of us can hear! What can we do to make him change his ways?

Bewildered and Hurt

Dear Bewildered and Hurt,
Don't waste time trying to change him; it's not possible. Put the television set in some other room for him, so the rest of you can carry on your conversation in peace, and don't worry about it any more. It's his loss, not yours.

Magic Granny

make plans around those limits. If it gets to be four o'clock, and they still haven't left, say, "Goodness, I was supposed to let you all go home at three-thirty, and I've kept you a half-hour past that already! We've been having so much fun that I lost track of the time!" And then start moving them firmly toward the door. Say things like, "Children, go get your coats, you mustn't keep your mom and dad waiting!" and "Do all of you have your car keys?" and "Can I help you carry things out to the car?"

This may not strike you as Gracious Living. It may be a startling break in family traditions. Never mind that. Your family will be forever grateful all the same. Grandmothers are not only the perpetuators of family traditions, they are the only people who can safely make needed *changes* in those traditions. So Great-Grandmother Charlotte always expected everybody to arrive right after breakfast and stay until dark, no matter how inconvenient and no matter how boring and no matter how dreaded it made the occasion. So what? She is no longer in charge of these things; *you* are. You have the right and the privilege to announce to your family that from now on things will be different, and to specify those differences. Furthermore, if the day comes when more changes are needed, you have the right and the privilege to do it again. Just say, "I have an announcement. Next year we're going to stop at half past two instead of three-thirty. I think that's best, and I know you won't mind." If you have a child rude enough (or a tiny grandchild unsophisticated enough) to ask you why, tell the truth: "By half past two I'm worn out, and a worn-out grandmother is no fun to be with."

While we're on the subject of family traditions, I need to warn you about something very important to a successful time-and-energy budget. Please be careful about setting precedents, because they have a tendency to become traditions! For example, when I had only two grandchildren I started making them crocheted Easter eggs. Beautiful things they were, too, with lots of intricate stitches and colorful embroidery, and rows of lacy ruffles . . . you can imagine. They took a *lot* of time to make. The kids loved them, their parents admired them, and I enjoyed both making and giving them. By the time I had four grandchildren, however, this had turned into quite a project. By the time I had *ten* grandchildren I had to start working on those eggs about the first of May to be sure I'd have at least one per grandchild finished by the following Easter, and I had nobody to blame but myself.

I now have almost no grandchildren who are still Easter-basket age. I'm coming to the end of Crocheted Egg Duty, and I am looking forward to it. And now, when something like crocheted Easter eggs takes my fancy, I make an announcement as I hand out the first examples. I say, "Now I want you to know that I may do this again sometime—and then again I may not. And if I *do* decide to do it again, I have no idea *when*." I make it very clear, for everyone's else's sake and for mine.

Be careful. You may assume that you'll never have more than one grandchild. Your offspring may be firmly convinced of it and give you their solemn word. But things change. Divorces happen; stepchildren happen; widowings happen. Many, many unexpected things happen. And there you are, keeping up a tradition for seven instead of for one! The wise grandmother keeps this in mind, and never has to listen

Keeping Track of Multiple Grandchildren

When you have only one or two grandchildren, the very idea that you might forget a birthday or a favorite color or a clothing size may seem shocking. But as a grandmother of ten, I assure you that with three or more you will find yourself forgetting these things. The wise grandmother will have a card in her telephone index for each grandchild—with full name, date of birth, clothing sizes, the name of each action figure or Barbie or other "series" toy already given to the child, hobbies and collections, and anything else that's likely to prove useful. Use a pencil for the items that will change constantly, like clothing sizes, and add new cards whenever they're needed. This is also the place to jot down messages such as "Melissa wants a tape player for her birthday" or "Timmy already has three sets of blocks—don't get him another one" before they slip your mind.

"Do you have a day runner to keep track of my grandkids?"

to half a dozen outraged young voices saying, "But you took Billy to the Grand Canyon! And you took Teresa to the Grand Canyon! It's not *fair!*"

🦋 Helping Family Members When It's Genuinely Necessary—and Still Staying Solvent

Every grandmother would like to be a fairy godmother as well, able to grant her family members' every wish with a sprinkle of stardust from her magic wand. Pumpkins into coaches, when your favorite granddaughter needs a coach, and all that. But this is the real world, not a fairy tale; stardust isn't available on demand. And to be frank, it wouldn't be a good thing if it were. The only thing more pathetic than adults who still turn to their mothers for every need like toddlers do and are entirely unable to stand on their own two feet is those same adults after Mother is gone. Don't do that to your children and grandchildren. Block that impulse. On the other hand, don't leave them to flounder when help is appropriate and you are able to provide it. Seek the middle ground, as always.

To be able to help out when that is right and appropriate, here are some nonmagical things that grandmothers can do.

🦋 Insurance Strategies

❖ Buy inexpensive term insurance policies in your own name at the earliest age possible, and make your children beneficiaries, so that when you die the money will be paid *immediately and directly to them*—without having to go through probate or be held up for any of the other legal proceedings that go with other kinds of inheritance.

❖ Whenever you are the payer of last resort for an obligation of one of your children or grandchildren, either as cosigner on a loan or because you are the lender of record and the child is making payments to you—for a house, for example, or a car—buy a term life insurance policy on the child, with *you* as the beneficiary. You do this so that, should the child die and leave you suddenly responsible for all the rest of the payments, you would immediately have money paid directly to you that will let you pay off that obligation without probate or entanglement in the child's other estate matters. (Note: If you cosign, you may be able to buy inexpensive insurance that simply pays off the note if either you or the child dies. But if you bought the house or car with the understanding that your child would make the payments by giving you the money for them each month, and you are the legal owner, that kind of insurance will be available only if *you* die.)

❖ Make sure you have health insurance and disability insurance for yourself, as well as home-health-care insurance, if you possibly can. You may feel confident that Medicare will take care of your health when you're older, but not only can't you be sure it will still exist when you need it, the amount of health-care money Medicare patients have to come up with themselves is getting larger all the time. It will do your kids and grandkids very little good if you fail to buy this kind of insurance because you want the money to buy them things, and they end up having to dip deep into their pockets to pay for your health expenses.

🦋 The Family Loan Fund

What do you do when your grandson says, "Grandma, if I don't put new tires on my car I won't be able to get to my job, and Mom and Dad say they haven't got the money"? Or your daughter tells you that a sudden dental emergency has made her unable to pay her mortgage this month? Or your granddaughter has saved enough money to pay for her week at camp but doesn't have any way to pay for the clothes she has to take with her? Or any of the other typical financial crises in the $50 to $1,000 range that are *real*—that is, that aren't the "But I *have* to have two-hundred-dollar sneakers!" variety of fake crisis?

You can certainly do what some families do: you can just say no. In the spirit of teaching kids to swim by throwing them in a river, which was the method one of my grandfathers swore by, you can refuse to help. You can say, "I'm sorry to hear you have that problem. I'm sure you'll find a way to solve it." This may be the best thing to do sometimes. It may teach self-reliance and hard work and character. But it may also mean watching your loved ones sink into the river and disappear without a trace. Setting up a family loan fund is one excellent way to avoid having to make this kind of difficult choice.

Early in your family's history, well *before* the first money crisis, open a savings account—in your name, because you're the grandmother—to serve as a family loan fund. The instructions that follow serve as an example and may not be exactly what you need, but you can adjust them to your own family's situation.

1. Every adult in the family chips in $10 for the first deposit; if that doesn't come to $100, you make up the difference. Every child old enough to get an allowance is also responsible for putting in $10, but is allowed to do it in installments of a quarter from each week's allowance for forty weeks (with the option of doing it faster by using birthday money, money from a part-time job, and so forth, if that's appropriate).

2. Every adult is responsible for contributing another $100 a year, on any schedule that fits. Kids can add more if they like but aren't required to; they're "fully vested" after that first $10. For this fund "adult" is defined as at least eighteen years old.

3. When your grandson urgently needs a new tire for his car because he can't get to work without it, that's a legitimate crisis. Instead of giving him the $50 to buy the tire, lend him $50 from the family fund, with the understanding that he will pay it back at no less than $10 a month for five months. No interest, no processing fees; he is just obligated to replace the money.

4. All crises being approximately equal, a family member who hasn't had a loan yet has priority over one who has. In cases where three people want loans at once and there's not enough money to cover them all, put three numbered slips in a bowl or a bag and let them each draw one to determine the order of the loans.

5. Encourage your family to do projects to raise extra capital for the loan fund. They can have a giant family yard sale, for example, with the understanding that all the proceeds will go into the loan fund.

6. The grandmother is in charge of this fund; people who want loans have to apply for them through her. And the ultimate authority for difficult problems that nobody foresaw well enough to write rules for in advance rests with the grandmother. In return for this authority, she will keep careful records of monies people put into the fund, amounts they take out, the payments they make on their loans, and any other essential data.

7. Anybody who abuses the fund will be given back the money he or she contributed originally and told to sink or swim—no more access to the family loans.

A fund like this, if sensibly looked after, will grow to be a useful resource, always ready for the clothes-for-camp and snow-tires and one-mortgage-payment kind of financial crisis. Everyone involved will be glad it's there, because it eliminates both the demeaning job of going to older family members and begging for money, and the very difficult job of deciding when to give that sort of help, whether to give or to lend, and all the rest of it. It can be tailored to every family's circumstances and customs; if it has to start with only $25, that's fine. If no bank will accept the amount you have available to start with, you, as grandmother, can hang onto the money until it has grown to a sum the bank will allow.

A family loan fund will teach even the smallest children about money. It's good for a child to try to justify a request for $25 for a new Barbie when she already has three Barbies, and to have to explain why that should be looked upon as a financial crisis. It's good for a child to

"We merged to save through volume buying."

learn that even though the account still has $100 in it he can't have any
of it because that's the lowest balance allowed by your bank. It's good
for a child to feel that he has contributed to the family's security and
well-being by agreeing to postpone a loan in favor of someone else
whose needs are more urgent. It's good for a child to understand that
borrowing money for legitimate purposes is not only not wicked but is
one way to make money do *work*. And it's good for a child to feel the
moral satisfaction that comes from having paid back a loan in full and
on time.

🕊 The Family Barter Bank

Money isn't the only resource, remember, and it's not the only way to
pay for things. Time and energy are also valuable, and can often be used
instead of money.

You may have heard about the barter banks that are being set up all over the country for elderly people, where one person does three hours of painting or gardening or typing or driving, and those hours are "banked" and can be drawn upon when that person needs a service. You can do the same thing within a family. A grandchild can do four hours' work around the house, cleaning up a basement or attic or garage, for example—anything that is needed and welcome, and that isn't a part of that child's regular chores—and those four hours will be credited to a barter account. Then, come the day that that grandchild needs four hours of someone else's time and energy to help with a personal project, those hours will be there to draw on.

It may be appropriate to set a value on the barter hours of youngsters who are too young to have regular jobs—$3.00 each, perhaps—so that barter could be used to repay money from the family loan fund if the kids get into a tight spot. But it must be understood in advance that the family will never put a money value on *adult* barter hours. There must be no chance that anyone will be asked (or allowed!) to decide whether the two hours that Aunt Grace spends doing Cousin Ned's income taxes are worth the same amount of money as the two hours Uncle José spends fixing Cousin Theo's car. Making such judgments is a good way to end up with a family *war*. ("What do you *mean* it's just as much work to hem curtains as it is to till a garden? It is *not!*")

The barter bank helps tremendously with the ever-present problem of who is or isn't being a martyr within a family. Everybody who gets something out of the system has had to put something in; everybody's efforts are considered equal; and nobody is doing things "for" any specific other person. Person A doesn't hem curtains or change spark plugs for Person B—Person A hems curtains or changes spark plugs for the family barter bank.

Children who grow up in a family that has a loan fund and a barter bank won't be shocked when they get their first real job and learn that they're expected to do an hour's work for an hour's pay—as long as these two family institutions are treated seriously rather than as a game. They won't learn a thing if they are given loans because their requests are so "cute" or if they are allowed to skip their loan payments because they're "just kids" and "too young to understand about such things." Putting the grandmother in charge makes it easier to avoid this kind of phoniness. The grandmother doesn't have to get up every morning and face the child who won't eat breakfast because she can't have yet another Barbie and her heart is broken by this tragic fate. The grandmother doesn't have to listen day after day to the teenager's frantic, "But I *can't* make a loan payment this month, I've got to buy tickets for that concert! I promise—let me skip just this one payment and I'll *never* ask to do it again! Pleeeeze!" And the chadults will be able to look at the kids and say, honestly, "I'm really sorry, honey, but your grandmother says no."

I can hear you thinking out there, "But my kids would just go behind my back and sabotage the whole thing! I *know* they would!"

That's possible. Let's consider it carefully, thinking like a grandmother. Suppose that what happens when you turn down the child's request for money to buy another Barbie doll is that her parents just go ahead and give her the money. In the first place, the parents who were so ready to hand over $20 for a doll will soon have to face demands for things like cars and trips to Paris from youngsters who take it for granted that the answer will always be yes. They'll pay for their sabotage down the road. In the second place, your grandchild will have two different models of behavior to observe and learn from, and that's a good thing. Many kids today grow up with no model except the one that tells them they're entitled to anything they want whenever they happen to want it. Children aren't stupid; given half a chance—and enough information—they will often make very good choices.

🌺 Explaining Resource Management to Your Grandchildren

Crying over spilt milk and water under the bridge is a great waste of resources; I try not to do much of it. But there's one such item

*". . . Then your grandfather and I invested in index funds
and lived happily ever after."*

that I want to share with you so that it will serve as a warning. I will
never cease to regret that I reached the age of forty—having worked
outside the home from the age of thirteen—without ever learning one
useful thing about business and finance. I was a college professor with
tenure and had a modest writing career on the side. I felt secure. It
never crossed my mind that I would find myself suddenly taking early
retirement for disability or that I would then be obliged to support my
family by starting a home business from scratch, *fast.* Things like that,
I thought—thinking like a youngster rather than like a grandmother—
happen only to *other* people. My ignorance about managing a business
and managing money was so profound that I survived only by blind
luck and the grace of God.

By the time I learned what I should have known all along, I had already let my children grow up in the same state of deplorable ignorance; it was too late for me to prevent that from happening. This taught me some valuable lessons. First among them was the absolute necessity of making sure that none of my grandchildren reached adulthood without knowing the business and money basics. It may be that in your own family these lessons are learned with lots of input from fathers and grandfathers; such help is always welcome. But if the men don't take this on, or don't do it adequately, be sure that you do it yourself.

It used to be that any moderately intelligent and presentable youngster could find work somewhere after high school, and as long as he or she showed up on time and did a decent job, steady progress and lifetime security were not only possible but probable. Grandmothers could sit back and watch their grandkids start in the mailroom and work their way steadily up the ladder to the limits of their ability, and be proud of them. It was just a matter of getting them through high school and making sure they absorbed the "work ethic" as they went along; then you could relax. *The world isn't like that anymore.* That day is long gone, taking with it the lengthy grace periods during which workers used to be able to get to know one another and learn to get along together.

Today there are only three reliable ways for your grandchildren to become successful and solvent adults who aren't dependent on either their parents or you:

* There's the old-fashioned classical track through law school, medical school, and so on. It costs an astronomical amount, both for education and for getting established in the professions, and all of them are now crowded and viciously competitive.
* There's the track of starting a business of one's own. That requires no official credentials, but it can be done only with a large investment of financial capital or intellectual capital, or both. And it requires a lot of self-discipline, with a willingness to work sixteen-hour days and seven-day weeks, often for years, until the business begins to have a solid foundation and earn a profit.

* There's the track of getting a job, as always. But today that means being able to move from task to task, project to project, at a moment's notice. It means being able to join a group of strangers and get along instantly. It means being always ready to change, always able to cope, always able to fit in, always able to communicate and adapt and be a member of any team whatsoever from day one.

This is why so many young people today are being referred to as "boomerang kids." Kids who can't follow any of those three tracks may turn eighteen, may turn twenty-five, may turn thirty, but they won't leave home for good, the way you did. They will keep coming back, because the money they're able to earn just doesn't stretch far enough to cover their needs. Sometimes it doesn't stretch far enough to cover their *children's* needs—and there you are, a grandmother with a family of three generations in residence.

Your children, the chadults, are caught in this bind, too, though perhaps not quite as tightly. Often, even if they're out on their own, they are too deeply involved in the struggle for simple financial survival to have any time or energy left over for seeing to it that their children learn how it's done. This is something you can help with. For example:

* Manage the family loan fund and the family barter bank, seeing to it that the grandkids participate fully in both and understand how they work.
* Give your grandchildren DayTimers (or any other brand of organizer), starting no later than their twelfth birthday, and encourage regular use.
* Play "stock market" and "bond market" (and any other sort of market you fancy) with your grandchildren. If you are a grandmother who prefers cooperative efforts, let the children help you pick a hypothetical portfolio that you all keep track of together. Check the market announcements in the papers and on television with them to see how you're doing and discuss what you should keep and what you should sell, what kind of records you have to have, how it

"Come on, show Grandma how smart you are—tell her the difference between a condo and a co-op."

would all be taxed, and all the rest. If competition is your style, let each one pick a portfolio to be dealt with in the same way, and see whose does best over time. If one of your grandchildren believes that investing in the collectibles or comic-book market is a better way to go, help the child try *that* out. Don't just keep track of it all on paper, though. Buy and sell and earn with lots of play money, to make it all seem more real. This will mean that by the time the grandchildren are adults they will know how the different types of investment work and what their jargon means, they'll understand the principle of making money *work* instead of letting it just sit around, they'll understand what an acceptable level of risk is, and they won't believe that lotteries and sweepstakes and casinos are the only road to financial security.

❖ Encourage your grandchildren to set up microbusinesses of their own, no matter how wild their ideas may seem. Buy them a copy of *Better Than a Lemonade Stand: Small Business Ideas for Kids* by Daryl Bernstein, and read it with them. When they turn twelve, buy them the current edition of *The Young Entrepreneur's Guide to Starting and Running a Business* by Steve Mariotti. Be willing to help them prepare a business plan, to be submitted to you so that you can consider investing your own money in their start-ups. And any venture capital you give them should be nothing like the family loan fund; it should be lent to them with an arrangement that will not only pay you back but earn you a profit on your capital if their business succeeds. Be willing to lose that money (being careful, obviously, not to invest more than you can afford to lose). And explain to them that many businesses *do* fail, but that it's no shame to fail when you've done your best.

❖ If you have Internet access, make sure your grandchildren go to some or all of the financial sites specifically for kids. They're very well set up, and offer valuable information in a form that youngsters can easily understand. My favorite three are Investing for Kids (http://tqd.advanced.org:80/3096/index.htm), Lemonade Stand (http://www.littlejason.com/lemonade/index.html), and Kids' Money (http://pages.prodigy.com/K/I/Y/kidsmoney).

❖ Be very interested and very active in your grandchildren's business doings. Ask questions; listen attentively to the answers. Report on their successes in the family newsletter. Never violate a business confidence; never make fun of an idea or an outcome. Make it clear that the ability to stand on your own two feet is something you value so highly that you're willing to really help them learn how it's done.

❖ Constantly, every chance you get, give your grandchildren opportunities to observe, and participate in, successful human communication—conversations, negotiations, presentations, and all the other interactions that are so critical to getting along in this world.

Finally, I cannot urge you too strongly to set aside the idea that only the grandsons need to learn these things. It's no longer true that girls need only learn to file and type because their future is a marriage to a man who will take care of them and their children all their lives long. Even if they make a good marriage, your granddaughters will probably have to work outside the home as well as in it, because few families today can get by on a single salary. Even if they marry men who are such good providers that they don't need to take outside jobs, your granddaughters are likely to have to be involved in their husband's financial affairs and the management of the family money. And no matter what their situation, it is a fact of life that many, many women suddenly find themselves divorced or widowed or in drastically changed financial circumstances, as I did; they really must be prepared for that possibility.

You should be involved in these matters not just because of your love for your grandchildren, although I hold that motivation in the highest regard. You should be involved because it's a crucial part of staying solvent yourself and of being able to enjoy your old age instead of spending it in a state of frantic worry about the financial problems of your progeny. It's worth every scrap of money and time and energy you put into it, simply for your own self-interest. All of it that you do for love as well is icing on the cake.

✴ Dealing with Family Greed

Ideally, you taught your children that greed is disgusting, and you did that so well that they have succeeded in teaching your grandchildren the same valuable lesson. When you give them gifts, they're pleased and happy. They don't feel that if a product exists they must buy it, just because it's there. They know the meaning of the word *enough*. And they are more than happy to share.

That's the ideal. In the real world, however, many things may interfere with the ideal. Your chadult may marry someone whose parents' most successful lesson was that only the greedy survive, setting the stage for a home where two opposing philosophies will be locked in perpetual combat. Or you may have raised a child who doggedly resisted your best efforts and grew up greedy in spite of everything you could do to prevent it. And now you find yourself with one of those grandchildren who, after opening a stack of presents, looks around and

When You Just Can't Stand It Any Longer . . .

There will be times when you'll be so angry, so disgusted, so frustrated, and so just plain outraged over some shenanigan by one of your family members that you're half sick. If saying so would accomplish anything useful, go ahead. Much of the time, however, you'll know it's a lost cause. In that case the thing to do is sit down and write a letter (or make a tape) in which you say every last word that you *feel* like saying to that person, in as much detail as you like. Don't hold back! Get it all out of your system, so that you can stop hearing it inside your head. And then: *destroy that letter (or tape) completely.*

This is like taking out the garbage and disposing of it properly instead of letting it sit there and rot. It's good for you, and good for your family, and good for the language environment.

says, "Is that all?" This is unfortunate, and heartbreaking, but it happens to the best of us.

The only thing you can do about this, frankly, is to set an example. Greed, like any other distortion of the spirit, is impossible to stamp out by force. Any attempt on your part to *persuade* a greedy family member of the error of his or her ways will get one of two reactions: that you are stupid and naive or that you are faking. Greedy people can't afford to admit the possibility that anyone who is intelligent and sophisticated might also be generous and uninterested in piling up more and more of everything. That would force them to come up with a good reason for their own behavior, and none exists. You're wasting your resources if you argue with such people; just go about your business of grandmothering and let that be your demonstration that they are wrong. As the years go by, they will come to understand that you are for real. You may not be so fortunate as to live long enough to see them change their ways, but you will probably have the chance to hear them say that they have come to *wish* they could. That's a start.

❧ Setting Your Own Affairs in Order So You Leave No Messes Behind

First and foremost, if you are wealthy you need the advice and assistance of a financial expert. By wealthy I mean that, without counting the value of your home, you are worth as much as $100,000, or that your home, even if it is your only real asset, is worth as much as $100,000. Many grandmothers who don't perceive themselves as rich women will meet those criteria. In that case, or anything roughly approaching that case, get expert help. It will be worth every penny it costs, and your expert will tell you what to do and how to get it done.

If that's not your situation, however, there are four things that you must do as thoroughly and completely as possible.

First, try not to leave a stack of unpaid bills. This doesn't mean you can't enjoy your charge accounts and credit cards. It does mean that it would be best to keep the number of cards small and the balances low, or to have insurance that pays all the balances automatically upon your death, or both.

Second, make a will. The mess that is created when people die without wills is made even messier by the fact that it's so easily avoided. Get an attorney to help you do this, so that what happens to your estate will be what you *intended* to have happen. Be sure that the will includes your wishes about burial or cremation, about a funeral service or memorial service, about organ donation, and about anything else of that kind that your family might need to know right away. Make sure that copies of your will are easily accessible upon your death—a single copy locked away in a safe deposit box that no one can open without a court order isn't helpful. Your lawyer should have a copy; your executor, if you have one, should have a copy; giving a copy to a trusted friend or associate or relative is a good idea. And in your personal papers, where your family can look immediately after your death, you should have a note (plus a tape or video, if you like) that tells them where those copies are.

Third, have an insurance policy that is large enough to cover such

D.R.I.P. Stocks

Many grandmothers are in no position to invest in the stock market in the usual way. Brokers will tell you that you should then invest in a *fund,* and that's one alternative. Another option—one they're less likely to mention—is buying stock in a company that offers a D.R.I.P. (direct reinvestment) option. For example, you can buy just one share of Johnson & Johnson—the baby powder people, a perfect investment for grandmothers—through a broker. You'll then get some material in the mail, including a form that lets you join the D.R.I.P. plan. From then on, without a broker and without paying any additional fees, Johnson & Johnson will let you invest $25 or more toward purchasing additional shares, whenever you like. You don't have to commit to any regular investment schedule; the company will help you with the paperwork and send you the necessary tax information; and the one and only rule is that you must invest at least $25 each time. You couldn't ask for a more painless or convenient way to build your wealth! (For a book that will give you much more information on D.R.I.P. stocks, with a list of companies and their requirements, see Charles B. Carlson's *Buying Stocks Without A Broker.*)

immediate expenses as your funeral and burial and your final utility bills, and that pays directly to a beneficiary you can trust to use the money for those purposes. It's hard enough on your family to deal with the shock and trauma of losing you, without their also having to try to borrow money for your final expenses while your estate goes through probate or some other legal rigmarole. Unless you have large and unusual expenses, a $10,000 policy would probably suffice.

Fourth, for heaven's sake leave instructions about how you want your belongings divided up! You can make an actual list, with the items in one column and the person(s) you want to have them in the other, and file it with your will. You can put a tiny sticker on the bottom of each item, with the name of the person you intend it for written there, and put a line in your will saying that that's how the dividing up should be done. I know grandmothers who say that they just can't do the dividing up themselves because no arrangement they can think of seems fair, or because two or more of their family members have asked for the same item and they don't want to choose between the two, or some such thing. In that case, specify *in your will* that your family has to list all your things on slips of paper that can be shaken up in a hat, and then everybody has to take the luck of the draw. Another possibility is the one that my family uses: each person selects one item in turn, until everything is divided up. (You may have to draw numbers for the first turn.)

However you want to do it, make your wishes known and make them clear. The only thing more distasteful than three surviving grandchildren fighting over your only piece of Wedgwood while your brother insists that *he* should get it is a family that auctions off everything you owned because they can't agree on who should get what and you didn't leave any instructions. Grandmothers should exit gracefully, and that means tying up this particular loose end, however irritating a task it may be.

Chapter 5

⊡

Emergency Procedures

❧ Thinking Like a Grandmother

To most young people every hint of trouble looks like an emergency. This is less because the young have no sense of perspective and proportion than because they lack experience. Over and over again, they have to deal with their *first* example of a given problem. Their first flat tire. Their first ticket for going 37 miles an hour in a 35 m.p.h. zone. Their first flunked major exam. Their first turndown for a job. Their first failed romance. Their first experience with a sick child. All those firsts have to be gotten through and learned from; it takes time. In contrast to this general tendency, there are young people who don't seem to have any crisis detectors at all, and whose troubles frequently descend on the rest of the family because no action is taken and no warnings are offered.

In either case, grandmothers know that the adage "This too shall pass" is true, and that most of the things we get agitated about aren't worth our agitation. (Not to mention the fact that many things that *do* merit distress turn out, over the very long run, to have been blessings in disguise.) The grandmother knowledge base that makes it possible to distinguish between the minor crisis and the real emergency is crucial to a family's well-being. The relevant Grandmother Principle, GP 14, is:

GRANDMOTHER PRINCIPLE 14:
SOMEBODY HAS TO BE THE GROWN-UP.

A great deal of the time, that "somebody" will turn out to be you.

❧ Real Emergencies Versus Phony Ones

In Chapter 3 we talked about how to proceed when a grandchild's parent is sick or injured and someone else—often a grandmother— has to take over the household. Such episodes are distressing and un- pleasant, but they're minor. However stressful they may be, however disruptive, everything goes back to normal once they're over. Real, major emergencies are different because they are events after which *nothing will ever be the same again.* We are incredibly lucky here in the United States; none of us alive today can remember a time when we faced war or famine on our soil, nor does either seem to be part of our probable future. Nevertheless, real emergencies are part of our lives.

Sometimes they are unquestionably catastrophic: your child dies suddenly, leaving orphaned grandchildren and a widowed spouse; a grandchild is born with a grave disability. Sometimes they are unques- tionably disgraceful: your grandchild is arrested for selling drugs; your married child is seen leaving a cheap motel with somebody else's spouse. Sometimes they are events that might not seem disastrous to outsiders but that, within the special context of *your* family, destroy some part of the family relationship forever: you ask your wealthy sister for a loan because one of your children is facing bankruptcy, the only time you have asked her for money in your entire life, and she turns you down flat. These crises, unlike minor ones, are events that have permanent, memorable consequences.

Every grandmother, like every other sane human being, longs for a

"Mrs. Redston, the doctor will see your pictures of your grandchildren now."

charmed life in which such things as these never happen. And real life certainly isn't like the soap operas in which the same poor soul is kidnapped on Monday, falls off a cliff on Wednesday, is railroaded into a mental hospital on Friday, and gets struck by lightning Saturday afternoon. Still, bad things do happen to all of us, and we have to get through them. And often the grandmother is the rock to which the rest of the family clings, even when her own pain is as sharp as theirs. You'd better be prepared for this, because it's inevitable.

🦋 How to Tell Real Emergencies from Phony Ones

There are people in this world (some of whom may be your relatives) who not only seem to thrive on crises but will deliberately *create* a crisis if none has come their way recently. Most of the time their "emergencies" are phony. That won't keep them from calling you up and wailing at you about their supposed plight. It won't keep them from calling sudden family meetings to make dramatic announcements or hijacking otherwise cheerful family gatherings for the same purpose. These people not only cause unnecessary distress for others, they put themselves in danger—because the day will almost surely come when they face a *real* emergency, and then their cry for help will get no response but, "Oh, not *again!*" (This demonstrates the importance of making sure your grandchildren hear the story "The Boy Who Cried Wolf" early and often. Presumably these people had grandmothers who neglected that task.)

Then there are the people (some of whom may be your relatives) at the opposite end of the spectrum: they're the ones who, with their house burning down around them, seem incapable of realizing that the situation is serious and something must be done, fast. In an ideal world your family wouldn't include either of these types; in the real world, you probably have one or the other, and you may well have both. You may have set the world's best example for your children as they were growing up, demonstrating to them how an adult reacts to events with just the right amount of alertness and alarm and not one scrap more, and yet you may find that you have a child who becomes hysterical over a chipped fingernail, and she has presented you with a grandchild who drives everywhere, serene as pond water, in a car with bad brakes. It's amazing.

You can't do much to protect family members who are oblivious to danger. You can be vigilant on their behalf. You can tell them when you believe that they should be alarmed. You can encourage them to get their brakes fixed. You can comfort them when things go wrong and they are bewildered as well as hurt. You can sit quietly and let them suffer the consequences of their lack of foresight, when those consequences strike you as tolerable, in the hope that eventually they will learn to make the connections. And then, having done all that you can do, you must leave them in the hands of Providence and refuse to let them monopolize your mind.

The Phony Emergency (PE) people are a different sort of problem. As a grandmother, you will have a full slate of real crises to deal with; you can't afford to waste your resources on phony ones. You need to be able to tell the difference. You can begin by asking four questions:

❖ Question 1. Is the PE person telling the truth about the physical facts? If the complaint is that the kitchen is on fire, are there flames and smoke? Has the fire department been called?

* Question 2. Is the PE person exaggerating? If there really is smoke, is it a cloud of smoke, dense and dark, or one small, pale puff of smoke from an oven that needs cleaning?
* Question 3. Did the PE person *cause* the crisis? As in being sued after sending an outraged letter of complaint about a neighbor to the local paper, with copies to every lawyer in the county?
* Question 4. If the PE person is telling the truth and is not exaggerating—and even if he or she is the direct cause of the crisis—is the emergency one after which nothing will ever be the same?

The first few times somebody will have to go check to find out what is really going on. When the answer to the fourth question is yes, something will have to be done, as with any real emergency, even if the PE person is entirely at fault. But when the answer to the fourth question is no, and the PE person consistently embroiders and distorts the facts, and/or deliberately creates crisis situations, it's time for you to call the senior members of the family together to decide on a policy for the future.

The decision could be that everyone loves the PE person dearly, pain in the neck or no pain in the neck, and that each alleged crisis will be given full family attention to the extent that that's possible. (This could only happen within a family, is one of the ways you know that a group *is* a family, and is one of the marvels that poets write about.) If that's the decision, set up a schedule as you would for any other sort of regular chore. Take turns! Assign two months of the year to each responsible family member. Do whatever it will take to spread the PE response duties around. There is no reason whatsoever for a grand-mother (or anyone else) to carry this weight alone.

The decision could be that the PE person's behavior is bizarre enough to require expert intervention, in which case steps should be taken to bring in a doctor or counselor or whichever expert is appropriate.

The decision could be that nobody in the family is going to take part in this nonsense ever again. That's harsh, but it may be the only sensible thing to do. It's not sensible, for example, for real family needs

to be neglected because everybody is constantly getting wound up in these phony crises. In that case, the PE person must be warned of the decision; that's fair. And you, as the grandmother, are the ideal person to carry the message.

Now, assuming that you've separated out the phony crises and are dealing with only the real ones, we can move along.

✣ What to Do While It's Going On

Whether the emergency is death or divorce or unwed pregnancy or drug addiction or something else, there are two important things that grandmothers can do.

First, there are often practical steps that will move matters along and lessen the stress. Usually they involve money. Money to pay a fine, to offer bail, to cover a medical or legal bill, to pay for temporary lodgings until an insurance settlement comes in, to pay for child care for a month or two. If you can afford to do these things, if you're willing to do them, and if you are sure it's appropriate for you to do them, go right ahead. If it's appropriate for the money to come from your family loan fund, that's even better.

Second, and in the long run more important, a grandmother needs simply to be available as a source of strength. You need to be someone whom every family member affected by the emergency knows they can come and talk to about their pain. Above all you need to be the person who will listen without moralizing and lecturing, without saying, "I told you so" or "How could you let this happen?" or "Pull yourself together, for heaven's sake!" It's not as if you were the only likely source of negative pronouncements like those. In every real emergency, other people will be coming around carrying those messages, both officially and unofficially. They don't need any assistance from you. Your children and grandchildren, however, do need you—badly.

This can be a very hard row to hoe; let's not try to pretend otherwise. When your son-in-law becomes a widower and his children are suddenly motherless, they all need your help. They need you strong and resolute and ready with comfort and a listening ear. But at the same time that they have lost a wife and mother, you have lost a daughter. There is no worse bereavement than losing a child, and you—and your husband—will be in agony. I have been through this myself, and I am here to tell you that it is awful beyond description. I can only tell you, as a grandmother, that your wisest move is to put the needs of the others first, if you can. That is not being a martyr. It is simply shouldering the load that you are better equipped to carry than others are.

If you *can't* do this, don't torture yourself about it. People have different degrees of strength and different tolerances for pain. If tending to your own pain is the limit of your strength, it's important to say so immediately, so that there can be no misunderstanding. Make it absolutely clear that you can't be any help to anyone else for a while, say that you are sorry, and then get out of the way. Understand that when you are in too much torment to function properly, for you to insist on trying to do more than you can do won't help at all; it will only add to the others' burdens.

Whatever happens, the only real source of healing is time. While time is passing, do what you can, because it's also true that staying busy makes the time pass more quickly.

🦋 What to Do When It's Over

People involved in emergencies sometimes have difficulty recognizing the various stages of the crisis. Sometimes they don't seem to realize that it's over. Pain in response to crisis is normal; mourning for what has been lost is normal; but the time comes when both must be given their proper place in the family's past rather than the present.

For all of the family, and perhaps especially for the grandchildren, what may be needed is a specific signal. They need someone to say, either in person or in a letter, that it's okay for them to stop living "on hold." It is a grandmother's proper role to do that. You can tell them that you know it's been hard, that you're proud of the way they have handled themselves and been part of the family support network, that you know they will never forget what happened, that you understand that nothing can ever be the same. And you can tell them that, with all that said, it's all right now for them to take up their lives again and go on to create a new kind of normal life tailored to their changed circumstances.

There's one more thing to remember in these dreadful situations: you must try hard not to do things that will interfere with the process of keeping that new life normal. This can be very difficult. You may have to draw upon reserves of personal strength you didn't know you had. Especially if, as most often happens, the bereaved spouse remarries. You are then facing the problem of what sort of relationship you will have with a person whom you probably cannot help perceiving as a "replacement" for your deceased child. The strategy of viewing the surviving spouse only as an acquaintance (which will seem natural to you if you and the child-in-law were never close) won't serve; you can't do that and still continue in the role of grandmother to the children in that household.

Let me give you an example from my own experience. My first husband died suddenly, very young, leaving me a widow with three small children; I later remarried and had another child. For the rest of their lives my mother- and father-in-law from my first marriage sent generous Christmas and birthday gifts to the three children of that marriage—but there was never a gift for my youngest child. When they came to visit, they took the three older children on wonderful excursions to lovely places—but they never took my youngest child with them. As they perceived things, our youngest was not their grand-child and they had no obligation toward him. Strictly speaking, they were correct. But my little boy was brokenhearted every time the other three kids went off for a day at a theme park or flew to Europe for a visit. I was able to work around the gift problem; I always bought gifts for him and put my in-laws' names on them, carefully forging their signatures. But there was nothing I could do about the way Ben was left out of all the excursions and visits, and each such occasion was a strain on normal life. It made my youngest different; it set him apart from his brothers and sisters; it brought up painful memories and kept them fresh; it was a source of tension and distress in our family life.

With all due respect, I must say that this was senseless. It would have been no great burden for my in-laws to add a gift for Ben to their Christmas box, remember his birthday, and invite him to join the other three children on outings. (I am happy to be able to say that my second husband's parents never favored their son's children over the other children; they were wonderful to me and wonderful to all the kids equally, and I honor them for that.)

Should you find yourself in this or a similar situation, I urge you not to make these distinctions between grandchildren and stepgrandchildren, parents and stepparents. It will be hard enough for your family to heal from the grief of their loss and go on with their lives without your creating unnecessary additional burdens for them. Hard as it may be, unnatural though it may feel, *for the sake of your grandchildren* you must do your best to accept the new spouse and any new children as family members. Let the new child call you Grandmother as the others do, and extend your grandmothering to that child as you do to your "natural" grandchildren. If the change were the result of divorce, you might have to worry about such matters as loyalty to your own child; when it is the result of death, you can set that aside and just let your grandmother heart guide you.

✤ Doing Triage

Life might be simpler if all grandmothers could occur in sets of threes; sometimes it seems as if just one grandmother cannot possibly handle the role alone. Consider the following scenario: Your husband has a badly sprained ankle and is in severe pain, and he needs you to drive him to and from his appointment with the doctor. Your youngest grandchild has chicken pox and therefore can't go to school, but his father is out of town on business and his mother has been warned that she'll lose her job if she takes any more time off from work. Your sister, who ordinarily could be called on to lend a hand, is taking her children to summer camp. And your mother, now in her eighties and frantic about her failing eyesight, has an appointment today with an eye specialist in a town sixty miles away—an appointment that she had to wait six weeks for—and needs you to drive her there.

This will not strike you as improbable if you are old enough to be a grandmother. Grandmothers today so often find themselves in this sort of multiple-duty web that they have been dubbed "the Sandwich Generation." On any given day they can and do discover that some crisis they *must* attend to exists for an adult child, their own spouse, and one of their own parents, all at the same time. When this happens—even when each of the individual crises is minor—the total situation is potentially an emergency after which nothing will ever be the same. Because these grandmothers have no choice but to turn down one person's (and maybe more than one person's) legitimate need for help, that person is going to be very angry and very hurt. That person is going to say things like, "You love X more than you love me; this *proves* it! How could you treat me this way?" (And your mother will add, "After all I've done for you!")

In situations like this, barter banks, formal and informal, are godsends. If you can call on some support network to take on one or more of the conflicting tasks, do that immediately and count your blessings. However, what if you can't? What if no one else is available to do any of these urgent tasks?

There is no right answer. To your daughter, your spouse, and your mother, there will be no question: your first duty is to take care of *their* crisis, and it's too bad about the others but that's just the way it is. You'd like to think that at least one of them would step up and say, "Obviously you can't do all these things at once! Let's just put *my* crisis on hold this time." If that happens, you have my congratulations, and it's a credit to your skill in all your roles—but it's not likely. Each of these people is too worried and too distressed to think rationally. You are fully justified in feeling that what you ought to do is flee to the Bahamas and let them find out how they like *that!* I know that feeling well. But assuming that fleeing is not an option for you, as it is not an option for most of us, here is what you will have to do.

To all of them you say, "The laws of physics, which I did not write, make it impossible for me to help all three of you at the same time. All your emergencies are real, and all are equally important to me. I love all three of you, and I can't choose among you. So here's what we're going to do. I'll put all your names in a hat, give it a shake, and draw one—and the one I draw is the one who gets first call on my time today." And stick to that. It won't be pleasant, but you won't have to listen to the charge that you chose one of them over the others, and you won't have to try to make that dreadful choice.

I can hear you thinking out there, "But that's so *cold,* so impersonal! I couldn't possibly do that!"

I agree with you that it's cold and impersonal. This is a situation in which there is far too much warmth and everything is much too personal. A cooling down, a detachment and a distance, can only be an improvement. But if it's true that you really could not do it, then you will have to choose between suspending the laws of physics and fleeing to the Bahamas, whichever is easier for you to accomplish.

"But there's *got* to be a better way!"

There should be, yes. If you know one, please get the word out to the rest of us as fast as possible! The only way I know to improve this situation requires that you tackle it long before it happens. From day one of your grandmotherhood, start building those support networks and banking those barter hours, even if at that point you can't imagine needing them. Then, come the day you find yourself sandwiched between and among a set of urgent needs, you will have a long list of people you can call on. You may still have to draw names to determine which crisis you handle yourself and which you delegate, but at least everything will be covered. It will be annoying and deplorable, but not tragic.

The prospect of multiple-crisis days like the one in the scenario makes some women decide they'd rather not take on that version of grandmothering at all. I understand that. It may be the right decision for you to make; you are the only one who can know. If so, you should immediately warn your family members that you're not willing to be the one responsible for their crises down the road. The more quickly you tell them, the more quickly they realize that *they* must build support networks, the better.

✿ Making a Tragic Event a Part of the Family Culture

This chapter has been somber up to this point, and necessarily so; its subjects aren't ones that inspire cartoons. It would be dishonest to write a book about grandmothering that didn't discuss the real problem of how grandmothers can deal with these matters. But we don't need to be morbid. There has to be a time for setting the somberness aside and bringing the laughter back, and that is something grandmothers may be better able to do than anyone else involved.

It's important to work the emergency, once safely past, into the story of your family. It's important to give notice that it's okay to talk about it by doing so yourself. That needs to happen. Tragedies that are never mentioned, never talked through, never made into stories, are tragedies that go on wreaking destruction long after they're over. They are like festering wounds, and will stay poisonous as long as they're not attended to. You can be the first one to start talking about what happened in a normal voice, the first one to introduce the name of a beloved person who has died into the conversation *routinely*, like any other topic of conversation. You can be the first one to tell the tale of the crisis with humor included. Sometime during the emergency something funny will have happened and no one will have dared laugh because it would have seemed disrespectful or worse. Grandmothers can bring up that part of the story and set an example by laughing about it. (For more about family history-making, see Chapter 7.)

You can also be the one who throws a party in honor of the parent who died, the child who had to be institutionalized, the family member who went to prison. Let everybody toast that person and say whatever they want to say about him or her. Encourage recollections and reminiscences, including all the angry ones. People will laugh and people will cry, and it will be very good for them to do both. I think it's a shame that most of us have given up the custom of holding a wake in circumstances like these. A wake is just what's needed and is probably what the person who is its focus would have wanted. Grandmothers may be the only ones in the family who feel safe proposing these badly needed celebrations, and they should do it, for everyone's sake.

❦ Dealing with Disgrace: Coping with Shame

When a family's dreadful experiences seem to come upon them through no fault of their own, the way sudden death or a birth gone wrong do, there will be support and sympathy from outside the family as well as from within. But when the disasters are due to criminal acts, to inexcusable negligence, to behavior that our culture looks down upon, the outside support won't be there, and guilt will be added to the burdens your family already has to bear. Grief is an emotion that people can face and work through and then set gently aside, perhaps with deserved pride in the way it was handled and the way its lessons were learned. Shame, the emotion that goes with being disgraced, isn't like that. It's very hard to be proud of having handled shame well.

I think the first thing you have to do when you learn that your fifteen-year-old granddaughter is pregnant or your grandson is addicted to drugs, that your daughter has embezzled money from her employer or your son has been charged with arson, is to sit down and tell yourself firmly, out loud, "This is *not* my fault; I am not responsible for it." You can't be of any help to anyone else until you've done that for yourself.

If you really are responsible, of course, you will know that, and you'll have to make peace with yourself as best you can; my heart goes out to you. But it's very unlikely! Even if you were a delinquent or criminal yourself once, it's still very unlikely. Look at any family with four children all raised in the same home by the same father and mother who set the same good example and meted out the same wholesome discipline. Some of those kids will be what you'd expect that kind of home to produce; some of them will go wrong at one point or another; and nobody will be able to explain why. Look at a family with four children who were neglected and abused by parents who set awful examples and whose discipline was brutish or absent; mysteriously, although some of those kids will head down sorry paths, some will turn out to be solid citizens. The upbringing a child receives matters enormously, but it isn't the *whole* explanation for the adult (or teenager) that that child becomes. The chances that you are responsible for the disgrace are very small indeed, and agonizing over that possibility is a waste of resources that neither you nor your family can afford.

As always, what matters most is that you make sure the offender knows that your love is as steady and sure as ever and that the rest of the family knows it too. You can despise the behavior and still love the person who carried it out; make that clear to everyone. And make sure that your grandchildren know that you intend to face the outside world with the same reasoned and steadfast attitude. You may not be able to hold your head up high and be proud of either the offender or the offending act, but you can be proud that your love can survive it all—if that is in fact true.

It may *not* be true, of course, in which case it's no good pretending. In that case you will have to content yourself with being proud that you do what duty demands of you, even if you can no longer love. No one in my large extended family has ever done anything that forced me to face this dilemma, thank heaven, but I can certainly think of offenses so unsavory that I might find it hard to love in spite of them.

Your grandchildren should be able to say, "Grandmother never pretended that she felt any love for our father after what he did—but she sent him a birthday card every year just the same, she wouldn't let anybody speak against him in her hearing, and she often told us stories about the *good* things Daddy had done." That way, they will know that you think it's all right for *them* to go on loving, even if you can't.

In the meantime, your family will have to live through the shame in the same way they would have to live through grief or any other painful emotion, and let time heal. Your strength and your good example will be indispensable to them while this is going on. You will need to say to them, "This is bad, but it is *not* the end of the world!" That is always going to be true; you're safe saying it.

One final note: Anyone over the age of fifty or so can look back at his or her life and see clearly that something they perceived as a tragedy at one time was actually, in retrospect, the best thing that could have happened. This gives grandmothers a useful perspective and attitude toward emergencies. But you should be extremely careful about trying to explain this to your family during a time of crisis.

Suppose you are asked directly, "Something like this happened to you once, long ago. How did you stand it?" It may then be safe to say that you can now see that what looked like disaster was actually a good thing. But don't say that unless you are absolutely certain it will help rather than harm. Chances are, your wisest course is to say that it was very hard, that there were times when you didn't think you could bear it, but that healing did come with time. "After all," you can say, "here I am!"

🦋 If You're a "Long-Distance" Grandmother

If you're a "long-distance" grandmother who can't go to the scene of the emergency and offer hands-on assistance, your role is necessarily going to be limited. That can't be helped; it's not your fault, it's the luck of the deal.

As always, let those on the scene know that if there is anything you *can* do, you're willing to do it. As always, send messages to the grandchildren to help them through the trying time. As always, avoid adding to the load—don't make constant phone calls to ask what's happening, for example, if people are going to be too busy and distressed to talk to you. If you are a praying person, by all means pray. Beyond that, it's out of your hands.

◙

Chapter 6

In Sickness and in Health

🦋 Thinking Like a Grandmother

We live in a society that constantly bombards us with the message that any time we're not comfortable—any time we feel so much as a twinge—something is terribly wrong, and that we're supposed to have perfect bodily comfort from cradle to grave. Should a twinge dare to intrude on us, we're constantly told, there's a pill we can buy that will wipe it out instantly; we should get that pill and take it right away. Commercials talk about pain "acting up," as if pain were some sort of badly behaved animal running loose in the house.

Grandmothers need to know that this is mostly nonsense. Twinges are a normal part of life, meant to tell us what's dangerous. Jabs and stitches and cramps and aches are there to give our bodies a language for expressing disease and telling us they need attention. Once we get past the childhood years, when many illnesses are for training our immature immune systems, most of our ill health comes from just four sources: hostility, loneliness, obsession with looking like a Perfect Person, and the side effects of medical care. The vast majority of health problems clear up on their own, given a little time. Grandmothers need to be able to distinguish between the real health problems and the mere nuisances, and grandmothers should provide a steady countermessage to combat the nonsense.

GRANDMOTHER PRINCIPLE 15:
NO SICKNESS OR INJURY IS SO BAD THAT
PANIC CAN'T MAKE IT A LOT WORSE.

People go to doctors for things that don't need doctoring, because they panic. They take pills—and go into the very dangerous places called hospitals—too soon and too often, because they panic. Sometimes it's the other way around: because they panic, because they're afraid of pain or expense or hearing a fearsome truth, they ignore a very real *need* for doctors and pills and hospitals. They tend to follow those same practices with their children—your grandchildren. They may be much quicker to let experts tack "disorder" labels on their kids than on themselves, because they panic. Where health and well-being are concerned, panic is our worst enemy, and grandmothers can often provide much-needed defenses against it.

Grandmothers know that almost all genuine emergencies will show themselves clearly. There'll be agony rather than pain that "acts up"; there'll be blood and high fever and broken bones and dreadful damage; or there'll be apathy—unnatural stillness and lack of interest. You'll know, if you're paying attention. The rest of the time, someone needs to stop and think, without panic, before doing anything. Grandmothers, because they've had a chance to see the same problems over and over again, can help both with the justified fear in the real emergencies and with the panic that comes from inexperience and believing everything you see on commercial television.

🕸 Defense Against First-Timer Panic

With my first baby I was embarrassed over and over because by the time I got to the doctor, quick though I was, Michael was obviously fine. All he had to do was sniffle or turn up with one little spot, and I was running for the phone to call the doctor.

I had a slim excuse or two for this. Those were the days when almost all jobs included generous health insurance that covered everything without question or quibble. I was a secretary; I didn't have to worry about being able to pay for medical care. For another, most of my life I've dealt with the consequences of having been a child who had polio for which nobody called a doctor until it was much too late, and I was determined not to let anything like that happen to *my* child. Still, I had to learn not to overreact.

You can't keep your grown children from responding to every spot and sniffle the way I did, although today's severely limited health insurance may make them a tad less hasty. You can share with them the following dozen core chunks of basic information about children and health.

1. Tiny kids get sick faster than greased lightning—and they usually get over it just as fast. *Everything* happens fast.
2. Injuries—broken bones, burns, hard whacks on the head, deep cuts, bites, bleeding, poisoning—are almost always obvious and need *immediate* attention. You need to be able to tell the difference between major injuries and minor ones and deal with the minor ones on your own. For the major ones, get the child to a doctor as quickly as possible. Chances for mistakes are high. Even doctors make them. It would be nice if a medical professional were always right at hand to keep those chances low. But most young families today have a hard time finding money for and access to medical care. Many injuries happen when doctors' offices are closed and an emergency room—or experienced older person—may be many miles away. They need a good thorough book on identifying and dealing with minor injuries. It doesn't have to be expensive, and it doesn't have to be new, just current, and with a detailed index in the back. And the important spots in that book should be marked with Post-Its the day it comes into the home, *before* anything happens.

3. A fever higher than 101°F (38.3°C) is rarely a good thing, but it doesn't mean as much in a baby or toddler as it does in an older child or adult. It takes infant bodies and brains a while to catch on to such things as regulating temperature. (That's true for the rest of their bodily functions, too.)

4. Most of the time, when babies and toddlers bump their heads it's not serious. There may be a huge swelling and a big bruise, there may be a little blood, there may be terrifying screams. Nevertheless, despite all the drama, infant skulls are soft and can take lots of bumps; if that weren't true, it wouldn't be safe to let them learn to walk. After a bump on the head, you want to watch for signs of trouble: vomiting, eyes that cross or won't track or otherwise look strange, a baby who can't be awakened, and apathy (see item 5). But in most cases it will probably be okay. What little ones *can't* take is having their brains bumping against their skulls inside. Never shake a child. Never.

5. The gravest sign of illness you're likely to see in a baby or child isn't fever or vomiting or spots, it's *apathy*. When the little one just lies there, won't turn to look when its mother speaks, can't be tempted even by a favorite toy or food or television program—then you may have real trouble. Try not to panic, because panic won't help, but grave alarm is fully justified. You need a doctor.

6. Babies and children aren't toys. People who throw them through the air, swing them by their arms, and perform similar shenanigans are asking for trouble and will probably get it.

7. Every household with children in it needs a book on baby care (such as the famous Dr. Spock book) with a section to which you can turn to find the typical symptoms of common problems, as well as the signals of great danger such as projectile vomiting (when vomit goes straight out or up instead of down) or a stiff neck that makes the child unable to touch chin to chest. Every used-book store has lots of copies of these books.

8. Children who complain of minor items like stomachaches or headaches and say they're too sick to go to school should be given the benefit of the doubt. But they should then have to go to bed and

Online Health Resources

* HealthAnswers is the best all-around source of health and health-care information online, in my opinion, and the easiest one to use. The address is: http://www.healthanswers.com.
* For problems that are more emotional than strictly physical, go to MentalHealth Net at: http://www.cmhc.com.
* For something very unusual, an excellent source is the Web site of the National Organization for Rare Disorders; it's at: http://www.NORD-RDB.com/~orphan. And you can reach the Office of Rare Diseases at: http://rarediseases.info.nih. gov/org.
* Many health conditions have their own home page, often complete with an online support group. To find it, just choose Directory Search from your menu and type in the exact name of the disease or disorder you want information about. Check out the items on the list that appears until you find a site that meets your needs.

stay there, and they should not—until you know what you're dealing with—be allowed to watch TV or be given stacks of toys to play with in bed. *Staying in bed sick should be boring.* The same is true for the child sent home by the school nurse with minor complaints; that child should go to bed and have a chance to be bored. A few days of boredom won't hurt a child, and kids who find out that pretending to be sick isn't going to be fun will give it up. (If a child has an illness or injury that requires a long stay in bed, that's different, of course. Then by all means bring on the toys and books and television!)

9. If you're worried about a child, call the doctor during office hours. Whatever the child has will *always* get worse in the middle of the night or over the weekend. Never worry about "bothering" the doctor. Being bothered won't hurt the doctor; if the doctor snaps at you, ignore it.

10. The most important part of health care for children is providing them with nourishing food, cleanliness, decent clothes, safety, vaccinations, and vast amounts of love. A child is more likely to be harmed by having a Coke and a Twinkie for breakfast every day than by a serious illness or injury.

11. Little kids need to be mildly sick once in a while. They have to get acquainted with the most common germs and bugs in their environment and learn to deal with them. They have to have colds, for example. If you could keep a child from ever getting sick, that child would become an adult—who usually can't afford to stay home in bed—with no defenses against minor illnesses. Be reasonable.

12. People who do the very best they can to look after their children's health and safety and who nevertheless see a child sick or injured should not agonize over it. They're human, and so is the child. It can, and does, happen.

✖ Grandmother's Principles of Medicine

This section (together with the twelve items listed on pages 139–42, of course) won't be as thick as your average medical textbook, but it will be no less useful and very much less expensive.

✖ Preparing and Administering Charms and Potions

Both charms and potions rely on the patient's own power to get well and get better, and urge that power on. Charms are verbal, and must always be administered with a calm and confident and loving voice. Potions are usually liquid and must be administered with elegance and aplomb.

The Best "Prescriptions"
Start with tiny amounts, in case of allergy!

✤ SYMPTOM	✤ REMEDY
Itching	Cornstarch
Nausea	Ginger (Health-food stores sell empty capsules you can fill.)
Diarrhea	Nutmeg (Careful! This works *very* well! ¼ teaspoon is plenty.)
Bloating	A baked potato, skin and all
Insomnia	Chamomile tea at bedtime
Pain	Music listened to through earphones (The earphones are essential—and much cheaper, and better for you, than bottles of pills.)

✤ CHARMS

❖ When something has to be done that will cause discomfort, like removing a splinter or changing a bandage, say:

This is going to hurt; I'm sorry about that. If it hurts so much that you can't stand it, you tell me—and I'll stop.

Almost always, by the time the child (or chadult) decides that what you're doing is truly unbearable, you'll be through doing it. In the rare cases when that doesn't happen and they do tell you to stop, you *must*, just as fast as you can. Otherwise the charm won't work the next time. Just stop as directed, wait a few seconds, repeat the charm (substituting "This is *still* going to hurt" as a new first line), and then start over.

❖ When you put someone to bed, for the night or for a nap, say:

You're going to feel a lot *better when you wake up, in my opinion!*

The "in my opinion" is important, in case this turns out to be false. You can then say, "I was wrong; even grandmothers are wrong sometimes. I'm sorry."

❖ When the child or chadult predicts disaster (for example, "This is going to make me throw up—I know it is," or worse), say:

That is very unlikely to happen—but if it does, I'll be here.

❖ When the reason for the sickness of body or spirit is something for which guilt on the patient's part is definitely in order, but the patient can't admit it, for some reason, say:

I know how sorry you are, and I know you can't say so, and I love you very much.

❖ When some improbable catastrophe (such as, "I *can't* go to school because underneath the playground there's a *snake* that chases little kids!") turns out to be the reason the child is claiming a stomachache, say:

I've been on this earth for half a century, and I have never seen a snake that chases kids, and I've never known anybody who did. If you come across one, you be sure and let me know right away, so that I can go take its picture.

Note: Children find "half a century" more impressive than "fifty years," "half a century and more" more impressive than "fifty-two years," "four decades—nearly half a century" more impressive than "forty years," and so on. These wordings *sound* grandmotherly.

❖ When medicine or a potion has to be taken, or when there's no medicine to give but the patient needs to have the feeling that *something* curative is being done, say:

I'm going to go get my special glass [or mug or cup and saucer] for you. I'll be right back!

See below for an explanation of this "special glass."

🦋 POTIONS

You need some equipment to use with your potions. I recommend the following minimum set, almost all of which can come from flea markets or yard sales:

- A very pretty, special-looking plastic glass
- A very pretty, special-looking glass glass
- An extraordinarily handsome mug
- An extraordinarily beautiful cup and matching saucer
- A very special-looking spoon
- A box of fancy drinking straws
- A jar of maraschino cherries

🦋 POTION ONE: Put ginger ale or any other fizzy soft drink (or Kool-Aid if you truly can't come up with something fizzy) in your special glass (the plastic one, if it's for a very small child or someone either weak or awkward). Add at least a maraschino cherry; add an orange or lemon slice as well if you have one on hand. Serve with a straw, either as is or along with the medicine to be taken.

🦋 POTION TWO: Make a weak herb tea—no caffeine. Mint is nice; also very nice is a tea called China Rose, available from many tea companies. (The effect on the patient of saying, "*This* is made with *rose* petals!" can be dramatic.) Serve it in the special mug or the special cup and saucer, with a bit of sweetening if that's indicated. Some tea companies sell honey sticks to stir with that are very powerful; a sprig of mint floating on top is also a good touch. Serve as is or along with the medicine to be taken.

Note: If you're doing this for an adult, you may want to use stronger tea or even coffee—tailor it to your patient.

🦋 POTION THREE: For capsules and pills, put the medicine in your special spoon along with a spoonful of jelly, jam, or marmalade.

If you might have to tend several people at once, you'll need more than one of each item of equipment. It's important to the children that these items be used *only* when they are sick or in crisis; otherwise their healing power will be greatly diminished.

🦋 Grandmothering from Wheelchair or Sickbed

Sometimes it won't be someone else who's sick, it will be you. Obviously you can't do much grandmothering if you're in acute crisis

"Libra (September 23–October 23): Busy, busy, busy. The accent is on excitement and romance. Be ready for a flurry of calls, invitations . . ."

Wellness vs. Helplessness

The biggest health danger you face—trust me—is one you may never have thought of: *deconditioning*. Don't let it happen to you! If you've always been desperately busy and suddenly find yourself with lots of leisure time, you may feel that you've earned the right to sit all day and read or watch TV or use your computer or do needlework or dream the time away. That's true; you've earned that right—*but it is a dreadful mistake to take advantage of it, and you will rue the day if you do it.* Go for a walk every day, or work in a garden, or go to the mall, or play tennis, or swim. Muscles and bones that aren't used turn into frail and useless muscles and bones. By the time you discover that your inactivity is no longer voluntary, it will be too late. For your own sake, as well as your grandchildren's, *keep moving!* The seven surest ways to end up helpless are:

❖ Don't have a pet.
❖ Don't keep a garden, of any size.
❖ Replace your live plants with artificial ones.
❖ Spend most of the day watching television.
❖ Move everything you need to the most convenient spot, so you never have to walk.
❖ Drive everywhere you go, and park as close to your destination as possible.
❖ Don't bother getting dressed unless you're going out.

yourself; nobody will expect you to. But many illnesses don't involve an acute crisis, and many go on long beyond that stage.

If you know you're going to be having surgery or be laid up for a while for some other reason—anything that will keep you from your usual contact with your grandchildren for a time—do some Advance Grandmothering. Suppose you expect to be out of the family loop for six weeks. You can write each grandchild three letters, one for every other week, and put them in stamped, addressed envelopes, ready to be mailed. Postcards instead of letters are okay; for young kids they're often better. Even in the hospital there'll be someone to drop off mail for you if it's all ready to go. Or make some tapes for the kids to listen to—read stories aloud or just chat, whichever you like—and get those ready to be mailed. If a grandchild's birthday will occur while you're under the weather, take care of that in advance too. Get the present, wrap it, and either arrange for it to be mailed or give it to the parents for delivery on the proper day, whichever is safer.

And what if you're taken ill suddenly, with no time to prepare? *Be* prepared. Early in the year grandmothers should address and stamp a few envelopes to each of their grandchildren; they should also get birthday cards ready to go. These should be kept in a box or drawer, along with items that can serve as presents in a pinch, as well as items carefully chosen because of an excellent price and/or because they're the perfect gift for a particular grandchild. If an unexpected illness or injury or medical procedure comes along, a lot of the advance work will already have been done.

It makes sense to avoid being out of touch with your grandchildren while you're not up to par; silence on your part would worry them, and it's usually unnecessary.

One thing that you should *not* worry about is how you will *look* if you'll be seeing your grandchildren during illness or injury. People in our society badly need a reasonably accurate image of sick people, especially elderly ones, and they aren't getting it.

There was a time when most people who were sick or injured were taken care of in their own homes, often with little or no outside help. When I was a child, children routinely went through the "childhood diseases," sometimes under quarantine. And most of us had been in many homes where an elderly relative lived confined to bed or wheelchair and was nursed by family members. We knew what sick people were like. Nowadays there are vaccines against those childhood diseases (which is a great blessing!) and the sick elderly tend to be in hospitals or

Your Gift Stash

Grandmothers need a stash of small presents that can be brought out in a hurry when needed and be put to good use for birthdays and other gift occasions. Keep your eyes open for things that your grandchildren would like when you're at a flea market or yard sale, or when you see a shelf of things on clearance; check those "99 cents or less" stores regularly. Be especially alert right *after* holidays. Watch for *sets* of items—dolls, cars, animals, seashells, art supplies, and so on—that can be taken apart [broken up] and used separately. For example, since I have four granddaughters, I watch for sets of small dolls, give one doll to each girl along with new (and all different) doll clothes that I've made myself, and keep one doll from the set so that I can add to the wardrobes in future and know that what I've made will fit.

nursing homes. As a result, most people—including, unfortunately, doctors and nurses just beginning their careers—have had little experience with anyone suffering anything much worse than a cold. (Remember this when you're baffled by the behavior of a brand-new medical professional; it will explain many otherwise baffling phenomena.)

If you feel like doing your usual makeup and hairdo and so on before sickroom visits from your grandchildren, that's fine. If you don't feel up to it, that's also fine. Not only won't it hurt your grandchildren to learn that a typical sick person is pale (or flushed) and haggard, perhaps a little untidy, it will do them good. It won't hurt them to find that children who jump on beds or run around the room screaming or make demands aren't allowed to be around sick people, and that sick people rarely feel like playing with kids. It won't hurt them to learn that sick people sometimes wince or moan, and that this is a normal part of life. They need to learn these things.

Your rule, if you feel like seeing the grandchildren, should very simply be: Don't frighten them. If you aren't sure you can remain reasonably serene—which still allows for the occasional wince and moan, even occasional tears—don't see them. If you don't feel *well* enough to have youngsters around, don't see them. If you can't trust the parents who bring them to you not to carry on during a visit, don't see them. Your letters or cards or tapes will fill in for you during your absence. Otherwise, let the children come. It will do them good.

There are a few questions you should anticipate. The four most typical ones, with suggested answers, are:

1. "Grandma, do you *hurt?*"
   * "Not very much, thank goodness."
   * "Yes, I do. And that's okay. People are helping me with it."

2. "Grandma, why . . . ?" (As in "Why does your face look like that?" or "Why is that tube coming out of your arm?")
   * "Because . . ." followed by an explanation suitable for the child's age and sophistication, keeping in mind the fact that many little kids today watch television shows about emergency medicine. Such children may very well ask you such questions as "Grandmother, when are they going to defibrillate you?"

3. "Grandmother, when are you going to be okay?"
   * "In about two weeks."
   * "I don't know. As soon as I find out, I'll tell you."

4. "Grandmother, are you going to die?"
   * "I don't think so; I certainly don't expect to."
   * "Everybody does die, you know, eventually, and so could I. But it's not likely anytime soon."
   * "People who have this problem do die sometimes—I know you know that—but I don't expect to."

And what if you really are going to die, and you know it, and your adult children know it? Should you say, "Yes, I am going to die"? That depends on many things: the age of the grandchild, the emotional stability of the adults around the child, family traditions and religious beliefs, and more. You will have to decide for yourself (in consultation with the adults, to the extent that that's appropriate) how to handle this most serious question.

My own feeling is that it's best not to lie to children about an *expected* death. When they find out that it's a lie, they will feel betrayed; and from that moment on, they will not trust any adult who tells them that someone's going to be all right. I think they have to learn that death comes to everyone, and that a death is as normal as a birth—everybody gets at least one of each. I think they must learn that the death of an elderly person, unlike deaths that come to younger people, is not only inevitable but appropriate. I believe that a grandmother is one of the best possible sources of this information. This is an opportunity to explain to children that although no one wants to lose a beloved person and the loss will be mourned, a death is the end of a life but not the end of the world.

🦋 "Taking to One's Bed"

It sometimes happens that grandmothers reach a stage at which they don't necessarily have anything seriously wrong with them but they can no longer function very well. (The better care they've been able to take of themselves, the older they'll be when they reach this point.) Often their only problem is a case of "the dwindles"—nothing serious, just weakness and tiredness and fragility.

When I was a little girl I knew ladies like this who were said to have "taken to their beds." Sometimes this meant actually staying in bed; often it meant staying mostly on a couch or in a big, comfortable chair or a wheelchair. Often these women were a lot of fun and a valuable resource. They had visiting times, sometimes every single day. Friends would come see them in midmorning or midafternoon. Everybody would sit and talk and laugh and drink coffee or Coke or lemonade, perhaps play cards, perhaps knit or crochet. Children, as long as they behaved, were welcome. It was like a salon or a party, and it wasn't considered tragic. I've known women who looked forward to it as they grew old and who thoroughly enjoyed it when the time came.

It's harder to do this today. Grandmothers are more often alone than they used to be, with nobody to look after them while they reign over the room from their bed or chair. When it can be managed, however, either at home or at the retirement center, I think it's an excellent idea. It's absurd for the grandmother who feels dizzy and weak if she's on her feet either to endure that feeling all the time (whether in silence or while complaining about it incessantly) or to give up all contact with the outside world because of it. Lie down, for heaven's sake, or sit down—whatever's comfortable. Let people know that that's how you plan to manage thereafter, and enjoy both yourself and them.

🦋 Growing Old Gracefully

M en in our society are allowed to age naturally, and the way they look is called "distinguished." If their cheeks start to sag and their necks start to raddle, they can wear a beard. Women don't have that luxury, and all our media and popular culture work to convince us that a woman who looks older than about forty-five is unpleasant to see and a burden to have around. *Grandmothers have an obligation to change this ridiculous and perverse attitude.* And not by trying to follow in the footsteps of the very rare woman who continues to look like Barbie till the day she dies, not at all! Grandmothers should seize every opportunity, when with a grandchild, to point out old ladies and call them beautiful. Like this:

> *You:* Look, dear—isn't she beautiful!
> *X:* Huh? Grandmother, she's all *wrinkled!*
> *You:* Yes, she is, and lovely wrinkles they are, too! You never see

wrinkles like that on young people—they haven't lived long enough to get any.

X: You mean it's supposed to be okay?

You: It's not just okay, it's beautiful.

It's important for you never to say things like, "Oh, look at these ugly spots on my hands, they're so horrible!" or "You're so sweet to take me places when I look so awful!" or "*Please* don't take my picture, I look so terrible!" As long as you live, *insist*—for the sake of humanity, as well as your own sake and your family's—that old women are beautiful. It's true, you know; they *are*. If more grandmothers would take it upon themselves to teach children about the loveliness of old ladies, our society would be far more wholesome. Raising little boys so that they grow up to be men who find old ladies beautiful is a project deserving of medals and large cash prizes; I urge you to give it a try.

The real secret of growing old gracefully has nothing to do with how you look; it depends on what you say and what you do. Here is a very basic list that, if followed to a reasonable extent, will keep your aging years from being "declining" ones.

- ❖ Refuse to go out if that tires you; have people come to you instead. If you do go out, be good company. If people *won't* come to you, don't let it bother you, and don't bother *them* about it either; it's their loss.
- ❖ Don't expect people to wait on you hand and foot. But when that can't be helped, be charming about it. That means never saying, "I know you hate to be with me, I know how you must feel, I'm *so* sorry. . . ." It means never saying, "You'll be old yourself one day, you just wait!" and never saying, "I'm a burden, I know I am." The appropriate things to say are, "How nice of you!" and "Thank you."
- ❖ Set up guidelines and stick to them, just as you did for family gatherings. Say, "Now that I'm seventy I intend to . . ." whatever it is that you intend to do.
- ❖ Eat what is served to you, without explaining how much better it

The Gramma Awards

Nana Novosel
Best Remake of an Old Standard:
"When I Was Your Age ..."

Mrs. Emily Branca
Album of the Year:
"Sit with Me a Spell."

Emma Lou Dill
Best Novelty Single:
"Every Doggone Bone in My Body
Hurts" b/w "Are We Living
in a Refrigerator?"

The Summer Ridge,
Virginia, Quilting Bee
Lifetime Achievement Award

Shanahan

would have been if it had been cooked the way you always cook it. It may be that nobody around you can cook decently—don't tell them so.

❖ When you're cold, put on a sweater or a shawl, or drape an afghan over yourself, instead of insisting on turning the heat up (or the air-conditioning down) to a level that makes everyone else miserable.

❖ When younger people say something outrageous about what they feel you ought to do or not do, try gently to dissuade them. If they won't hush, just let them exhaust themselves, and then say, "I hear you."

Growing Food

You may not have room for an entire garden; you may not want to fool with one (see page 94 before you decide). There are things you can do to make your table more spectacular, all the same. Put up a fluorescent light (the kind often called a shop light) above a shelf or other flat surface where you can put some plants in pots. (You don't need the fancy, expensive "grow lights"; fluorescents serve the purpose very well.)

This will let you grow herbs in pots; oregano, chives, and basil are especially easy. And there is a magic cherry tomato that not only *can* grow indoors under lights but is hard to keep *from* growing! It's called Sungold; the seeds produce delicious little red or orange tomatoes (your choice). It's as easy to grow as dandelions, and a single plant in a big pot is plenty for one person. Mine provides me with fresh tomatoes all year round, year after year. Sungold seed is available from Johnny's Selected Seeds (207-437-4301; 1 Foss Hill Road, Albion, ME 04910-9731; homegarden@johnnyseeds.com) or Thompson & Morgan (800-274-7333; P.O. Box 1308, Jackson, NJ 08527-0308).

You can start more basil and oregano—and Sungold tomatoes—and present the new plants as gifts. Just cut off a nice, sturdy chunk of the plant (something you'd have to do anyway, because plants do tend to get too big for the space you have available) and put it in a jar of water under your fluorescent lights. When it has sturdy roots, plant it in a pot of good potting soil and pass it on. (You've probably done this with philodendrons; it's exactly the same procedure, and just as easy.) If you're not much for growing things from seed, start by buying one basil or oregano plant, and from then on just cut off a chunk to start a new one for yourself whenever the current plant begins to tire.

The World's Simplest Lunches for One

❖ With a microwave: Put two cups of cooked rice in a soup
bowl. (Wise grandmothers cook a pot of rice at the beginning
of each week and keep it in the refrigerator, to be micro-
waved at a moment's notice.) Add some chopped raw vegetables—some tomato, some onion, whatever else you have on
hand. Don't hesitate to add some leftover cooked vegetables;
they'll blend right in. Add basil or other herbs, to taste.
Dampen a paper towel, squeeze out the excess water, and
place it over the top of the bowl, smoothing the edges to fit.
Microwave five minutes; salt and pepper to taste. It's ready.

❖ Without a microwave: Drain a small can of tuna and put it in
a soup bowl. Add chopped raw vegetables—tomatoes, onions,
peppers, whatever you have on hand. Herbs are nice, if you
have them. Mix gently. Pour a quarter cup of lemon juice (or a
bit more or less, according to your own taste) over it all, and
mix gently again. It's ready.

- Don't greet people with, "How long can you stay?" and don't send them off with your complaints about how short their visit was ringing in their ears.
- When people wish you a good morning, don't answer them with, "What's *good* about it?"
- When people tell you their troubles, don't answer them with, "You think *that's* bad? Let me tell you what happened to *me!*" When they tell you their accomplishments, don't answer them by topping their story with an accomplishment of your own. And never, never say, "When you're *my* age, my dear, you'll understand. "
- Have temper tantrums only rarely, make them brief, and after they're over say, "Goodness, I'm glad *that's* over, and I'm sure you are, too!" and then change the subject.

Grandmothers, even very young grandmothers, *are* going to grow old. Doing that gracefully is just another way of teaching by example and is well within your capabilities.

Chapter 7

◘

Mythmaking and Story Telling

There is no Grandmother Principle that says, "A grandmother always tells the truth." Nor should there be! Many of the most important things a grandmother says will not be factually true, and the true/false distinction will often apply to them in a new and different fashion. Still, grandmothers are expected to teach their children and grandchildren not to lie, and to set a good example along those lines. This requires some explanation (and some fancy footwork).

✖ Thinking Like a Grandmother

People who are not grandmothers tend to divide all narratives into three groups: Lies, Boring Drivel, and Entertainment. In the lies group they put "I can't possibly bake cookies for the Halloween carnival because my stove is broken." In the boring drivel group they put, "Let me tell you what happened to *me* this morning. I got up right before six and I took a shower—I always do take a shower first thing in the morning because it wakes me up, you know? Don't you think it does? Especially when the water is nice and hot? And our water *is* hot, you know, since we put in that new water heater. And then I had just started to make my toast, on wheat bread—I *always* use wheat bread for my toast—when . . ." (and so endlessly on, detail after stupefying detail). In the entertainment group they put everything else that isn't strictly factual, like the narratives in books and films.

All myths are stories, but not all stories are myths. And it causes much confusion that one common meaning of myth *is* "lie," as in: "You think all French people are great cooks? That's a myth." We won't be using the word that way in this book. What makes a narrative a myth from a grandmotherly point of view is that if it's true, that's fine, and if it's false, that's also fine. As Tony Jones puts it in an article called "God and Scientist Reconciled," a myth is "a fictional storyline which acts as a vehicle for the real information you are trying to get across." Worrying about whether a myth is true or false is like worrying about whether a Ford Taurus is true or false.

The tale of George Washington chopping down the cherry tree and admitting that he'd done it—"Father, I cannot tell a lie, I did it with my little hatchet"—isn't true. It's a myth; somebody made it up. That's all right. Its purpose is not to preserve the factual history of the United States of America, but to teach children a larger truth—that great Americans don't lie about what they've done, even when telling the truth means getting punished. The story is a parable that happens to have a real person for a main character instead of just beginning with "Once there was a little boy who cut down a cherry tree." It is a demonstration that one good way to teach a child to speak the truth is to tell a story about telling the truth that is itself *false*. Thinking about this without the steadiness of a grandmotherly mind would make you dizzy.

Deciding when a larger truth is more important than exact historical facts requires great wisdom. Let's consider a typical issue about which a grandmother would need to make such a decision.

Suppose your brother Terrence, who died in his early thirties, was actually a pompous and spiteful bully whose company everybody dreaded. Those are the facts, and there may be lots of stories about Terrence that demonstrate them. It takes a grandmother to decide which of the following should be what the children hear about Great-Uncle Terrence:

*"... and your great-great-grandfather lost the race,
but then it was discovered that the tortoise was on steroids."*

* The unpleasant stories based on historical facts.
* A silence intended to let his memory fade gracefully away into the shadows of time.
* A myth that goes something like, "Your Great-Uncle Terrence played the banjo better than anyone else I ever knew," with appropriate details.

How do you decide? Well, we don't insist on telling little ones that Santa Claus is a myth, because we agree that Santa Claus serves a purpose in our culture that's more important than the "true facts." We know the time will come when the children will be old enough to hear those facts along with an explanation and that they will then understand and approve. You treat Great-Uncle Terrence the same way.

Would the cold, hard facts about your brother weaken the family bonds or cause useless pain? Would a myth featuring his skill with a banjo fill some family need? Then let the man be of some use to all of you for once! Let him star in the myth of "Terrence the Fandangous Banjo Player." You can set the dreary facts down in writing somewhere for adult posterity, with an explanation of your reasons for sugar-coating them; meanwhile, Terrence will be pulling his weight at last.

🎵 Why Myths and Stories Matter

Much careful research has made it clear that almost everything we do in life is structured by stories. Our minds have to deal with millions of items of information from the world around us every single day. We have to decide which items we can safely ignore, which ones are okay to notice and then forget, and which items we have to index for our long-term memories. We have to do things to make our remembering possible. The sheer number of choices facing us, if we had to consider every single one individually, would be so overwhelming that we wouldn't dare get out of bed in the morning!

Stories help us make sense of all that by structuring our experience for us. They help us understand and learn; they sort things out for us. They may also entertain, fill otherwise empty time, make a point, present family history, or just calm things down around us; they may be suitable for a more long-term purpose and get promoted to the status of myths. But above all they guide us through the otherwise terrifying flood of experience.

Stories are also valuable because they let you deliver necessary messages in a way that is more effective and more likely to be listened to and remembered. When the choice is between saying flatly, "Plan ahead or you'll starve!" and telling the story of the ant and the grasshopper, the story wins every time. It's no accident that the great religious teachers put so much of their teaching into parables. Stories just *work* better for holding a listener's attention and getting important points across.

A family's own set of stories and myths ties the family together.

It says to children, as they come along: "This is how our family structures and understands what we experience. This is how we make sense of things. This is how we know what matters to us and how to set our priorities." The better the set of stories and myths is, the more effectively it will serve those purposes—and the less your family will flail about, getting nowhere.

Now there is a Grandmother Principle that we need to bring in to close this section.

•••
GRANDMOTHER PRINCIPLE 16:
THERE ARE SECRET STORIES THAT ONLY
GRANDMOTHERS SHOULD KNOW.
•••

By the time you get to be a grandmother, you will almost certainly know at least one batch of family facts that are as unsavory as spoiled fish—and you will probably be the *only* one (other than the persons actually involved) who knows them. People will tell you things they'd never think of telling anybody else; you'll find yourself alone with people who are dying or demented and who don't realize that they shouldn't be saying what they're saying. In soap operas, women hear that sort of tale and immediately rush off to tell half a dozen of their closest friends; that's one of the reasons why the average family in a soap opera goes through two kidnappings, a murder, and a bankruptcy every single month.

In the real world, women have better sense than that. Grandmothers have to have the wisdom to decide whether such secrets should go into family stories and myths, or go with you untold to your grave. When there is any question in your mind, the second choice is the right one.

This isn't always easy—I do understand that. Like any grandmother, I know some family stories that, if generally known, would break hearts without accomplishing anything of value to balance the heartbreak and justify it. Sometimes knowing such things is a burden; there are times when I feel that if I don't tell them I'll explode. That's normal. When it happens to you, you should be neither surprised nor alarmed. But be aware that the feeling of impending explosion is temporary and that the temptation will pass. *Wait it out.* Keep the terrible secrets to yourself.

Note: On the off chance that you really can't manage to hold your peace and *must* tell someone, tell a professional. We call our professional listeners therapists, and keeping our secrets is one of their professional skills.

🦋 Managing the Family Story-and-Myth Collection

The younger adults in your family are busy, tied to full schedules, still trying to get ahead and make a mark in the world, still doing most things on a short-term basis. They're usually not well suited to managing your family collection of myths and stories. You are, and you can do it like a breeze.

🦋 Collecting Stories

Some stories will fall into your lap, for free. You'll see them happen, or hear about them, or come across them in a book or other medium. Other stories you'll have to hunt for—you'll need a narrative of a certain shape and kind and you'll have to either find one to fit or make one up. Fortunately, there's such an abundance of stories that can be borrowed from the collections in libraries (both print libraries and electronic ones) that you'll rarely have to create them from scratch. If you aren't familiar with that abundance, just go to any library and tell a librarian you'd like to look at some collections of stories; that will get you started. The key to collecting stories is paying attention—being alert for them in the world around you and being sure to write them down or record them while they're clear in your mind.

Books for Grandchildren

- ❖ Call or write for the **Chinaberry Catalogue**, 2780 Via Orange Way, Suite B, Spring Valley, CA 91978, (619) 670-5200. It's nothing like an ordinary book catalog. More than a hundred pages long, it features long, detailed reviews of books for children from many publishers, sorted for you by age level and subject, with indexes to help you find what you need instantly. It also includes information from parents and others about the way *children* react to the books. No grandmother should be without her own copy of the **Chinaberry Catalogue!**

- ❖ For an *annual* list of "best of the year" books for kids, and a list of books recommended especially for reading aloud, write or call the Children's Book Committee, Bank Street College, 610 West 112th Street, New York, NY 10025, (212) 875-4540, and request a catalog of their publications.

𝕸 Tweaking and Polishing

Two things matter when grandmothers add stories to the family collection: *plot*, which is a familar term, and *euphony*, which may be new to you. For grandmothers, euphony is the one that's important.

When writers create stories that have to be sold to readers, they worry most about plot, because plot is what sells these days. But grandmothers' stories are usually going to be either stories already created for children (like "The Three Bears" and "Bambi") or stories about things that have actually happened in your family (such as "Why Aunt Jamaica Set the Barn on Fire"), and they arrive with their plots already in place.

Euphony has to do with the way language *sounds*. To call a story euphonious means that it's delicious-sounding. Whether you're telling stories to small grandchildren—who will listen to almost anything—or to far more critical older grandkids and relatives, euphony is the grand-mother's most essential tool for story telling. Always go for euphony.

When you collect a story it often won't have precisely the plot, or exactly the euphony, that you need. In such a case you are free to tweak and polish until it's qualified to go into your collection.

Tweaking a plot means making a minor adjustment that does the story no violence. You take a children's story in which the main charac-ter is a little boy named Billy, but because the grandchild you're telling it to is named Joshua and he's feeling left out at the moment, you open with "Once there was a little boy named Joshua." You take a story about a family dinner at which somebody threw up (through no fault of his or her own), and you leave that detail out of your telling. A story that is about two kittens would be a better story with three, so you add one. That's plot tweaking.

Tweaking for euphony will change nothing much in a story except the sound of it. You do it to make the sound of your words, and the tunes and rhythms you set them to, more nearly irresistible. For exam-ple, this sentence is a typical opening line for a family story: "My sister Amy was born in April." Here are half a dozen ways to say that more euphoniously:

- ❖ "My sister Amy, bless her heart, was born in April."
- ❖ "My sister Amy was born in April—a very cold and a very *dreary* April."
- ❖ "My sister Amy, light of my mother's life, was born in April."
- ❖ "My sister Amy, poor little thing, was born in April."
- ❖ "My sister Amy was born—just a *tiny* little bit of a thing!—in April."
- ❖ My sister Amy was born—much to your great-grandmother's sur-prise—in April."

You see (and hear, in your mind's ear) how that's done? It's like the trimmings we add to music to keep it from being just one chord after another. We put in runs and trills and little extra warbles—embroideries

A Zipper Lullaby

A zipper song is one into which you can always "zip" new lines as you need them, on the spur of the moment. For singing to babies, I recommend "Goin' Down the Road Feelin' Bad," with very minor tweaking. Like this:

"Best little baby in this whole wide world!
Best little baby in this whole wide world!
Best little baby in this whole wide world, lord, lord!
Your grandmother says it, so it's true!"

"Too much candy's sure to ruin your teeth . . . (3 times)

"I don't think you ought to eat that frog . . . (3 times)

"Winifred is such a pretty name . . . (3 times)

You see how it's done? Just zip in whatever suits your needs, and finish it off with "Your grandmother says it, so it's true!"

and embellishments—in between the chords, to get us from chord to chord more pleasantly. "My sister Amy was born in April" is your set of basic chords.

If you have a natural gift for euphonious tale telling and have perhaps been holding yourself back because you thought you needed to tell your stories *faster*, glory in your skill and put it to use. Time is a very subjective thing, as anyone who's ever compared five minutes at the dentist with five minutes of a romantic interlude can testify. The time you spend telling a story will be perceived as going by faster if the story sounds delicious—even if, measured by the clock, it takes longer.

If euphony doesn't come naturally to you, a little practice will fix that. Take any story you know well. Sit down with it and add embroideries and embellishments. Tweak it gently. Not "One day your Aunt Jamaica set the barn on fire" but "One day—and what a *miserable* day it turned out to be!—your Aunt Jamaica set the barn on fire." Or "One day your Aunt Jamaica, bless her heart, set the barn on fire." The best way to hear how you sound, so that you can decide whether you're satisfied, is to tell a story or two to a tape recorder and then listen to the tape carefully. If you bore *yourself*, the chances are good that other people will feel the same way. In that case, more tweaking is needed. Never mind modesty; polish the story until, when you listen to yourself telling it, you are enchanted.

Preserving Stories and Passing Them On

The family collection of narratives belongs in your family newsletter, in your family history (see the next chapter), and—so that you can be heard telling at least one or two—on cassette tape.

Throwing Myths and Stories Together, Using Only What You Have in Your Mental Refrigerator

You'll find many stories already written and told that will be perfect for your needs; it's hard to improve on "The Three Little Pigs." But grandmothers have been in this world so long, have been through so many experiences, and have observed so many other people's experiences! They have a vast amount of raw material available that's ready to be put to use and too good to be allowed to go to waste. One of the great regrets of my life is that I was so slow to realize this that I didn't encourage my own grandmother to share her stories with me, and many of them are lost forever as a result.

Using that raw material, grandmothers can find their family's unifying tales and symbols and metaphors, weave them into stories and myths, and tailor them specifically to the family's needs.

As a way to get you started, I'm going to take a story from my own experience and show you how it was turned into a tellable tale.

"Gram was actually alive during art deco, weren't you, Gram?"

Here are the bare facts, in the form of a list of items from my own store of raw material.

Just the Facts

1. When I was eighteen and newly married, my husband and I went to spend a summer with his parents, who lived in Geneva, Switzerland. I was an unsophisticated girl from the Ozarks; my husband was used to a very different lifestyle.
2. One night we went out to dinner with some of his family's friends, including an elegant woman who was a Russian diplomat and was wearing a light-colored summer dress.
3. I ordered chicken. I thought it would be fried chicken, to be eaten with the fingers, which was the only kind I'd ever known. But they brought me a roasted half-chicken.
4. When I tried to cut the chicken it flew off my plate and into the Russian diplomat's lap.

5. A waiter came, took the chicken away to the kitchen, and brought it (or another one like it) back to me. I tried again to cut into it—and the same thing happened!

6. Once again the waiter took the chicken away and brought me more chicken; but this time it had been cut up into tiny pieces the way food is prepared for toddlers.

7. Through it all everybody pretended that nothing had happened—it was horrible.

That's the historical truth, but you probably wouldn't want to sit and listen to it. Now let's take the bare facts and tweak them slightly, both for plot and for euphony.

🦋 Just the Story

When I was eighteen years old and newly married, my husband and I went to visit his parents in Switzerland. I was a gawky girl from the Ozarks then; Geneva was as exotic to me as the moon! And the first night we were there we all went out to dinner with some very elegant people—including a high-ranking Russian lady diplomat in a dress of ivory silk.

I ordered chicken, thinking surely that would be safe. But the only kind of chicken *I* knew anything about was *fried* chicken; the bird the waiter brought me that night was roasted, not fried, and definitely not finger food. And when I tried to cut it with my knife and fork it flew *off* my plate, *clear* across the table, and *right* into the Russian diplomat's lap!

A waiter removed that chicken of mine, took it to the kitchen, and brought it—or a new bird just like it—back to me. But when I tried again to cut it, I did it again! I know how unlikely it must seem that such a thing could happen twice, but I give you my word: Off the bird flew again, into that lap of expensive ivory silk!

Once more the waiter took the chicken away, and once more he brought it back to me. But *this* time the meat had been carefully removed from the bones and cut up into stacks of neat little bites, the way you'd prepare meat for a tiny child.

Through it all, and through the endless time I spent eating all those little squares of chicken, it was as if everyone else in the room had gone stone blind. No one laughed. No one looked. No one spoke of it. No one, not even my husband, so much as raised an eyebrow. I was as invisible in my havoc-wreaking as a *ghost!*

It was absolutely *horrible.* I wanted to die on the spot. But I didn't. Here I am—still alive—to tell the tale.

The truth is, I don't really know that the Russian diplomat's dress was white silk, much less ivory silk. But "a dress of ivory silk" sounds wonderful and offers superb contrast in the mind's eye when a chicken is added to it. The truth is, I don't remember if this happened the first night my husband and I were in Geneva, only that it was very soon after we arrived. But that detail isn't important to the story; "the first night we were there" is more dramatic than "soon after we arrived" or "early in our visit"; and saying, "I don't remember exactly when it happened, but . . ." is boring. So I always say it was the first night. And when the story-telling situation demands high drama, I have been known to make the Russian diplomat an ambassadress! You've heard of poetic license; this is grandmother license.

What if I were challenged by a meticulously picky and precise grandchild or chadult? We all know people who do that sort of thing, and some of them may be related to us. They say things like, "Are you *sure* it was really the very first night?" and "How can you be *sure* it was ivory silk?" If they were there on the occasion you're telling a story about, they say things like, "Well, I'm not at *all* sure it was ivory silk, myself!" If I were challenged in that way, I would explain it exactly as I have explained it here. And finally, in my family history I would take care to explain all of this in a footnote, meticulously, for the record.

I have used this chicken-and-ivory-silk story for decades, whenever someone in my household was distraught with embarrassment over having made some public mistake. It usually goes something like this:

X: Nobody has *ever* done anything so stupid in public before in the history of the world! I'll *never* be able to hold up my head again as long as I live!

Me: Honey, I did something once that was an awful lot worse than what you did.

X: That's impossible! You couldn't have!

Me: It's possible. Believe me—it's possible.

X: Really?

Me: Really.

X: (Dubiously) What did you do?

Me: When I was eighteen years old and newly married . . .

Similarly, faced with an account of dreadful circumstances, I always explain that my way of getting through a mess is to tell myself, "Well, at least I'm not on a train headed for Florida with three little kids—one still in diapers—who've all just come down with chicken pox on the train." Followed by *that* story.

It really happened. My husband was in Europe visiting his parents, without me—perhaps as a result of the chicken episode—and I had to get from Kansas City to Sarasota with the kids by train, all by myself. We were no more than twenty minutes out of Kansas City when the spots began popping out on all three children. The conductor quarantined me and my loathsome brood in a roomette. You have not really traveled until you've spent three days shut up in a roomette under those circumstances. Ever since, whenever I've caught myself thinking, "I can't *do* this!" I have stopped and run through that chicken-pox-on-the-train tale in my head and decided I could manage. And all my childen and grandchildren have learned from that story to say to themselves, "Well, at least I'm not on a train headed for Florida with three little kids—one still in diapers—who have just come down with chicken pox!" and get on with whatever it is that's complicating their lives.

I want to stress, while we're here, that the point of stories like these must never be "You think *you've* got problems? Let me tell you what happened to *me!*" It must never be "Hey, one day you'll look back at this and laugh!" Whatever trouble your family member is facing seems enormous to him or her, and it's a serious mistake either to top that problem or to trivialize it. The point is to explain that it's possible to live *through* whatever the young person is facing and come safely out on the other side. And the point of doing it as a story instead of just lecturing about it is that stories are infinitely easier to listen to—and to understand and remember—than lectures.

When grandmothers make sure the family stories are well known to everybody, they don't always have to be told (except to new arrivals, of course). The first line of the story will often be enough. Sometimes just a reference or a reminder, a dozen words or so, will do it. One of my chunks of raw material is a camping trip during which, as I was having a blissful time and enjoying myself enormously, I suddenly realized that the actual living conditions of the trip were identical to those of a "natural disaster," but that I had no desire to be rescued. It was all a matter of how I chose to *perceive* things. I've made sure that that story has been carefully passed along and well understood. As a result, for my family the question "Wait a minute . . . Is this a disaster, or are we only going camping?" is enough to make everybody stop and take a fresh look at our circumstances with an open mind. It doesn't take the whole story to bring that about. And I can be sure that as my daughters go on to become grandmothers they will hand that story on down through the generations—because it is so useful and saves such a lot of time.

People who aren't grandmothers might wonder why there's any need to go to the trouble of doing things this way. Why not just say what you have to say, straight out, and be done with it? But grandmothers know better: All you have to do to be *heard* is just be loud. Getting people to *listen*—and remember—requires that you be *interesting*.

Chapter 8

◙

Recording Your Family History and Passing It On

❧ Thinking Like a Grandmother

The *idea* of a family history has the seductive allure of those stately
British movies in which people dress formally for dinner every
night and have rose gardens and no one is ever in a hurry. You think
of a thick leather-bound volume with "The History of Our Family"
stamped on it in 24-karat gold, and inside, written in an elegant hand,
without a single blot or blemish, every last family detail, going all the
way back to the Crusades. Lovely, you think. And then the reality
buzzer goes off in your head. And you say to yourself, "I must be losing
my mind!"

Chances are, that leather-bound masterpiece is as unlikely in the
life of the average grandmother as dressing for dinner is. But that does-
n't mean you can't put together a family history for your children and
grandchildren to treasure. It's just a matter of making a few adjustments. The relevant GP:

GRANDMOTHER PRINCIPLE 17:
IT WILL BE FINISHED WHEN IT'S FINISHED.

Think of the difference between a football game and a game of chess. You can't start a football game at two o'clock one afternoon, play for fifteen minutes and quit, come back to it three days later for half an hour, and continue in fits and starts until you reach the end of four quarters. A chess game, on the other hand, can go on for years; the chess pieces will sit right there waiting for the next move, for as long as it takes. Nongrandmothers, living with tight schedules that involve not only their own personal deadlines but those of others, are often forced to tackle projects as if they were football games. Grandmothers rarely have to do that. Which means that projects that might otherwise seem too large and difficult even to think about become manageable: they'll be done when they're *done,* that's all, and if that doesn't happen to be in your lifetime, the world won't end.

"Do you remember any of those things people said we'd tell our grandkids someday?"

A family history is one of those projects that, if you think of it as something to be done in Football Mode, seems impossible. All those people; all those dates and places; all those little bits of data! All those stories that must not be lost because they're crucial pieces of the family culture quilt! The solution is just to start your history, work on it as much as you like *when* you like, and not worry about it. Someday it will be done, and every chunk of it you finish will be valuable.

To make this work, however, you need to use a system that makes that style of work possible. If it takes five minutes for you to find your history-in-progress, ten for you to set it up, and another five to put it away, you're in trouble. You'll feel that you can work on it only when you have at least half an hour's worth of information and time and energy. This puts an artificial barrier between you and the task. There will always be a reason for feeling that a particular moment doesn't quite qualify as a good time to work on it. It has to be totally convenient and instantly accessible. I'll tell you how to manage that.

❧ Why a Family History Matters and Why a Grandmother Should Be in Charge of Getting It Under Way

Suppose your oldest child is under thirty. Ask most people that age whether they care about having a record of their family history and they'll tell you no, they don't. "Why would I be interested in all *that* stuff?" they'll say as they're heading out the door or pulling away from the curb.

But give them a few years—the exact period varies from one chadult to another—and they'll be calling you up and asking very different questions. Like "Wasn't there somebody that used to take me to the swimming pool when I was three, and he had false teeth, and his name was Ernie?" And "Didn't we have a car, when we were living in Decatur, that had blue-and-white checked upholstery?" And a lot of questions that start with "Whatever happened to my . . ." followed by things you've long ago thrown away or given to the Salvation Army.

This change comes about when your children pass a sort of temporal divide and suddenly become aware that they have a Past and a Future, and that both have *limits*. Up to that point they've been concerned only with the Present (except for ritual future events like being old enough to drive), and they have considered their personal present to be limitless and eternal. When they wake up to their own mortality their attitude changes, and they will reproach you bitterly if you can't deliver. You'll protest and remind them that they said they didn't care about such things, and they'll tell you fiercely that it was your responsibility to know that they'd change their minds one day.

That's not fair; how would you know? But now that you've read it here, you do know. I give you my word, they're going to want all those details. The older they get, the more trivial the details that will matter to them, and they will treasure the information you can provide. They may still not want to hear it told— because good listeners are rare, and lots of family stories have weak plots—but they'll want it recorded somewhere and available to them. They'll want to take up the record where you leave off with it, too, and because they have your example to go by they'll know how to do it. You might as well get started.

••

GRANDMOTHER PRINCIPLE 18:
GRANDMOTHERS PLAN FOR THE LONG HAUL.

••

I'm well aware that not all of today's grandmothers live in nice houses with well-tended lawns surrounded by peace and quiet and order. Many of you live in places that are crowded and noisy and dangerous. You may have the sorry luck to be grandmother to youngsters who take it for granted—with good reason—that they'll be lucky to survive their teens without getting shot or stabbed or run over. I also know that you may be a grandmother who isn't forty yet yourself.

Neither of these factors means that a family history project isn't for you. On the contrary!

What you must understand is that in such situations the family history is even more desperately needed than it is for families living in less difficult circumstances. You can't clean up the mean streets for your children and grandchildren, but you can give them a reason to want to come *inside*. A family history will show them that they belong to something, something that stretches over generations. That's a gift of tremendous value, and one that is uniquely yours to give.

You grandmothers are the best people to undertake the making of a family history, for the obvious reason that you've been part of the family longest and remember it best. You are also someone who can look at it from the point of view of a historian. That is, when you reach the point in the history where your sister Alice lost your favorite sweater on top of borrowing it without asking you, you don't become so furious about it all over again that you can't even write it down. You're able to be detached about such matters and set them down for the future without calling Alice all those names you called her at the time.

🦋 Getting It Started, Keeping It Going

🦋 What You Need

You need a big three-ring binder, something to write with that won't fade the way pencil writing will, and a supply of paper. Paper with lines on it and already punched to go in the binder—like ordinary notebook paper—is best, but any paper will serve. That's it. You can get the binder for less than a dollar from Quill Office Products (see page 33 for their mailing and e-mail addresses and phone number.)

🦋 What You Do

The key to this project, the one thing that will make it work simply and easily for you, is: *Everything goes in alphabetical order.* Seriously.

You don't want to set up your history like the store-bought variety, in which somebody has decided for you that you need three pages for family christenings when your family has never had one, and provided only one page for family pets when you need at least six just for the dogs. You're not going to worry about *chronological* order, slogging along from January to December year after year as if you were recording the Napoleonic Wars. Every item you put into your history will go in sorted by the alphabet.

Suppose that one morning somebody goes by wearing a scarf that reminds you of the Mrs. Johnson who was third-grade teacher for you and three of your siblings. You will only have to decide whether to put the note you write about Mrs. Johnson into the Js for Johnson or the Ts for Third Grade (or for Terrible Teachers, or Terrific Teachers), as you like.

It's important to put every entry you write on its own page of notebook paper. That's not being wasteful; it's just thinking like a grandmother, planning for the long haul instead of for the passing moment. You don't want to suddenly remember a wonderful tale about Cousin Esther and have nowhere to put it because it would have to go after "Edward's Lost Goat" and before "Eternal Hope Cemetery" and you've left no empty space between them. Furthermore, you want room to add more details as they come to you. And they will, I promise you. The entry that starts out only two sentences long, all alone in a sea of empty paper, will turn into a full page when you remember something you'd forgotten or find an old clipping that gives you details you hadn't known about before.

Yes, this will eventually mean a lot of pages; it may mean that you'll eventually need more than one notebook. So? That's not a problem. Having to leave good things out because you don't have space for them is a problem and will spoil the project for you. Having to copy things over again to move them to different spots is a problem and will turn the project into tedious hard work. Put each item on a separate page and avoid both of those unfortunate consequences.

When you keep your history alphabetically in a loose-leaf notebook that you can get to easily, with every entry on its own page, this project is a piece of cake. You can write a line here and a paragraph there and put it in the notebook whenever the fancy strikes you, without effort. You can carry a few sheets of paper with you at all times, so that you can do an entry or two when you have to sit in somebody's waiting room or somebody's traffic jam. You don't have to worry about what you write when, or about finishing one item before you work on another one, or anything else of that kind. As I said—a piece of cake.

🦋 Two Variations

You can of course use exactly the same alphabetical order technique and put your history into your computer instead of on paper. That's fine, if it's as easy and convenient for you as a notebook would be. It's not fine if matters are so arranged that it takes you lots of time to start up and shut down, or if you can only use the computer at certain times. It's not fine if you forget to back up your files and then lose them when your equipment crashes. It's not fine if your computer's not portable and you can't take it with you. I write my books on my computer, but I prefer paper for my family history because I can't type at night without disturbing others; you may not have problems of that kind.

There's one other way: you can put your whole history on cassette tapes. Some grandmothers dislike both writing and typing so much that they'll avoid the whole task if they have to do either one. I understand that; there are things I avoid with the same determination.

Tapes do have disadvantages in this case. You can't riffle through them to see what's there or find the story "Edward's Lost Goat" quickly. Tapes can't be scanned and pored over the way paper or computer files can. You can't scribble a quick note in the margin to add something you suddenly remember. You can't easily run off a dozen copies of tapes the way you can photocopy sheets of paper; copying tapes is more expensive, more complicated, and takes a lot of time. Most unfortunate of all, tapes aren't convenient for you to use. Putting a story about a teacher into the Ts will take a lot of fast forwarding and rewinding and retaping and futzing around.

Even so, with all that said, a history on tape is an enormous improvement on no family history!

....

GRANDMOTHER PRINCIPLE 19:
IF IT CAN'T BE DONE ONE WAY, IT
CAN BE DONE SOME OTHER WAY.

....

If you are someone who can't tolerate writing or typing, you go right ahead and use your tape recorder, and never mind the drawbacks.

🦋 Plan A and Plan B

You can't know in advance how detailed your family history will turn out to be or how large a part your own life will play in it. You therefore need Plan A and Plan B.

For Plan A you have just one history. Its title is "The Story of Our Family," and when you write an item about your own life it goes right in there with all the rest. In Plan B you have two histories. One is called "The Story of Our Family" and the other is called "The Story of My Life," and you file things accordingly. Which brings us to another advantage of putting your work into a loose-leaf notebook: you can change your mind, effortlessly. Suppose you start out feeling that you couldn't possibly need a separate notebook for the story of your own life *("What, me write an autobiography?")*, and then find to your surprise that half of what you write is about you. That's fine. You just take out all the autobiographical pages and put them, already in alphabetical order, into a notebook of their own. No harm is done, and no problems are created.

"It was my great-grandmother's bathing suit. I keep hanging on to it, but I have a feeling it's never going to come back in style."

❧ Optional Frills: Bells and Whistles

What I've described so far is more than ample. Still, you may want to expand it somewhat. For instance, you'll probably want a photo album or a box of photographs to go with your history. That's an excellent idea. Just be sure that you always identify every single picture! I have a whole box of family photographs that I treasure but that cause me great frustration because nobody still living can tell me who some of the people shown in them are.

You might think that it's not necessary to write careful notes, such as "This is Melissa Carpenter in 1969 with Will Roy Smith, who drove a truck for your Uncle José; the dog just wandered into the picture by accident." After all, *you* know all that, and writing the notes is a nuisance. But not only will your offspring not have the necessary information, the day is likely to arrive when Melissa and Will won't look familiar to you either, or you won't remember their names. Write the notes, feeling perfectly free to scribble them down any old way that's decipherable. Information, not elegance, is the point here. You'll be glad you did it, later.

It's also useful to have a box for what is called memorabilia. Into it you throw things like your first pair of shoes, a child's first lost baby tooth, the postcard you bought the time you went to Chicago when you were nine, and so on, along with similar items you've collected from other people in the family. As with your photographs, you'll want to identify everything clearly, in order to avoid altercations like this one:

You: I can't *believe* you threw that baseball cap away! How *could* you?

Chadult: But it was falling to pieces—I thought it was junk!

You: Junk? *Junk?* I'll have you know, your *father* gave me that cap! On our *first date!*

Chadult: Well, how was *I* supposed to know that?

You: [Tight-lipped, icy silence.]

Chadult: Well? *Well?*

The easy way to do all this identifying is to write your notes about Melissa and Will and your first pair of shoes on Post-Its—those little sticky notes that have become as necessary to human life as bed sheets—and attach them to the photo or object with some of that "magic" tape that doesn't tear things up.

This may sound to you like wasteful duplication of effort; it's not. You use the Post-Its because they are so quick and so convenient, and because you can stick them on the wall (or any other nearby surface, including your elbow) to keep them from getting lost or mixed up with other stuff. You use the tape once things are in their final locations because over time the Post-It stickiness does wear off. You don't want to leave your family a box of historical items with a small pile of loose Post-It notes lying at the bottom, faced with puzzling out which note went where. If you are the sort of meticulous person who can cut tiny perfect notes out of scrap paper and attach those with rubber cement instead, more power to you, of course, but Post-Its and tape are easier.

Now here are some more possible extras, definitely frills rather than necessities, that might appeal to you:

* Add one of the commercial "Grandmother Remembers" or "Our Family" books, nicely filled out with no mistakes because you were able to copy everything out of your notebook. This one can be laid out on the coffee table at family get-togethers for people to pass around and leaf through; it's a display item. And it solves the problem of what to do when your family gives you one of these store-bought books, "So you won't have to make do with that crummy old *notebook* any longer, for crying out loud!"

* Ask everyone in your family (everyone who's old enough) to write you a letter on a subject of your choice—"The Best Christmas [or Hanukkah or Kwaanza or Cinco de Mayo or other occasion] I Ever Had," "The Teacher I Liked Best," "My First Job," "What I'd Do If I Had One Million Dollars"—that sort of thing. Tell them you don't care a bit about literary quality or spelling or grammar, you just want them to write down what they'd say if they were talking to you. Then collect all the letters and put them into a notebook of their own.

  Do this only *once*, mind! When a new person marries into the family or a child reaches the proper age, it's fine to ask for a letter to add to the collection. If you keep asking for more letters on more subjects, however, your relatives will dislike you intensely for it and avoid any contact with you that might give you a chance to assign them more chores along this line. And they will be right.

* Chapter 1 gave you the instructions for producing a family newsletter with ease and speed (see pages 31–40). If you decide to do that, putting one fresh, clean, unwrinkled copy of each issue in a notebook labeled "The Smith Family Irregular" is a nice touch.

❖ Do make a cassette tape—just one, so that it's not a chore. Choose one or two family stories that you know (from previous testing) are enjoyed and listened to willingly, and put them on tape with a label that tells listeners what to expect. It will please your family to be able to hear those two stories in your own voice, forever.

🦋 Handing It All Down

The day will probably arrive when you'll want to drop your history keeping, either because you feel you've gone as far with it as you can or because you've simply decided not to do it any longer. At that point you'll be faced with a decision: do you turn it over to someone else in the family, or do you keep it right where it is until you die? A number of arguments for hanging on to it will occur to you:

❖ *"They'll only get peanut butter on it!"* So what? Consider the sums of money that advertisers spend to "involve you" in the sales pitches they mail out—little stickers to lick and put on the order card, little colored dots to punch out, coded cards in hard-to-open foil packets. They do that because massive research proves that people who are allowed to wade into a mailing and do things to it *care* more about it and are more likely to buy. The same thing is true of your family history. It will matter more to your descendants if they're allowed to wade right into it, peanut butter and all, and make it their own.

❖ *"They'll only write in it!"* If you mean that your family members will use it to add up their bills in, you're right to be outraged. But suppose you mean they will add to its *contents*. Perhaps even circle the spot where the peanut butter is, and write beside it, "This spot is from the time when Johnny was only four and he used to sit and look through this notebook by the hour and pretend he could read it." Or "This is Grandmother's version of the argument we had about the lost goat—but it's not what really happened. What really happened was . . ." Again, so what? This is a *family* document, and part of that family's heritage. The more information it contains, even when some of it contradicts other parts of it, the more valuable it will be to your descendants.

❖ *"They'll only lose it!"* No they won't. Not unless you've rushed matters. If you turn the history over to them while they're still in the "Why would I care about *that?*" stage, they may indeed lose it. That's not their mistake, it's yours. Wait until you start getting those phone calls asking family history questions before you make the transfer.

❖ *"They'll only sell it!"* This is a different problem entirely. For your family to take the history you've written for them, perhaps over the course of decades, and sell it would be despicable! It's also very unlikely. It might happen if you are a famous person or if you have such a gift for writing that you've turned what started out as a private project into a book with wide public appeal—but it's very unlikely.

However, there's one thing all grandmothers need to keep straight in their heads if they want to keep their sanity:

··

GRANDMOTHER PRINCIPLE 20:
AFTER YOU GIVE PEOPLE SOMETHING,
IT BELONGS TO *THEM*.

··

You will drive yourself to distraction and despair if you start putting conditions on gifts! As in, "This is yours, provided you polish it every week and dust it daily" or "This is yours, if you promise to take care of it the way your father always took care of it." A gift with strings attached is not a *real* gift. Anything that you can't bring yourself to give away string-free—and that includes the family history—is something you should keep.

🌿 The Solution to All These Problems

You may not be able to face the peanut butter and the refutations of your versions of events in any serene fashion, even if you aren't worried about the other two potential disasters; I can understand that perfectly. There is a graceful way to handle matters if you rightly feel very attached to the family history notebook because you've looked after it all those years, and although you love your family you don't trust them to look after it in your place. You proceed as follows:

1. Make as many copies of the pages as you want and put each set in a notebook, to be given to whomever you choose. (If you do this, it would be wise to make a copy for each household.)
2. Keep the original, right where it is.

That's your privilege. Absolutely. What the family needs is the information the notebook contains, and that's in the copies. Not to worry.

There's just one more objection to undertaking a family history left, and I'd like to close this discussion with it. This is the objection most likely to come from *you*, the one that goes, "But if I do that, it will be a *mess!*"

The first time I ever started a family history I wasn't thinking like a grandmother, and I let that objection bother me. I'd write what I thought was all of some family tale, filling the page, and then I'd remember a crucial item I'd left out. I'd be excruciatingly careful as I wrote a page, and then I'd read it over and find three errors. I'd forget to be careful at all, and spill my coffee on the page. I'd misspell things and misnumber things. And then I'd try to fix it, but the ink remover and liquid paper and the like would only make matters worse, so I'd grit my teeth and throw it all away and start over again!

It took me a while to realize that even if I started over five hundred times my family history would not be perfect. And that I was turning what should have been a pleasure into torment by trying to be perfect, when perfection had nothing to do with the task at all. Think about it. If you, right now, had a notebook of your family history prepared by your own grandmother's hand, and it had lovingly done crossings-out and additions above the line and the occasional coffee splash, would those imperfections spoil it for you? Of course not!

Don't start over, then, once you've begun. Don't worry about the corrections and additions and changes you need to make; put that effort and energy into adding more new things instead. The more such imperfections your history has, the more it will be truly *yours* and the less it will be like something churned out by a machine. And that's what matters.

❧ If You're a "Long-Distance" Grandmother

Keeping the family history will in some ways be easier for you, simply because you won't be interrupted as often by your children and grandchildren. On the other hand, *current* history will be harder for you to keep track of because you won't be there as it happens.

You need what journalists and editors call a stringer—one or more persons to send you the news, at least in "bare facts" form. You may be able to get the chadults to do this, or you may need to rely on older grandchildren. My own success in this regard varies wildly, although all my children were raised in the same fashion. I have one chadult who can always be relied on to let me know about anything newsworthy, complete with photographs and memorabilia; I have one who checks in perhaps twice a year, never sends pictures, and—despite having e-mail as I do—might as well be on the moon. And I have everything in between those two extremes.

All you can do is make sure that your family members know you're eager for their news. To increase the chances that they'll help out, send them cameras and film and batteries, if necessary; send money for developing the pictures, plus self-addressed stamped envelopes for returning them to you. You can't *oblige* relatives to help you with the history-keeping task, but you can reduce the number of excuses they have for not doing so.

◘

Conclusion

✵ Thinking Like a Grandmother

Remember the first line I quoted to you, many chapters ago? "In most traditional cultures," it said, "grandmothers are people of immense importance and authority." Now that we're approaching the end of this book, it will be very clear to you why that is so—and why it should be just as true for our own "less traditional" cultures as well. *Grandmothers matter enormously.* They are the safe havens and solid foundations of the family, and have been so since the beginning of time. To be a grandmother and fulfill that role is a great honor, and *deserves* great honor.

We know this with even more certainty today, because anthropologists have recently announced the answer to "the evolutionary puzzle of why postreproductive human females, alone of all the primates, live so long after menopause." They live to a ripe old age for the sake of the family and the grandchildren, Sidney Callahan reports in *Commonweal*. While doing research with peoples still living as hunter-gatherers, scientists have discovered that it is the food-gathering skills and activities of the grandmothers that determine the weight gain of weaned children and that provide mothers with the time they need to look after the rest of the family. We now have good evidence, Callahan says, that "grandmother power" is probably what's responsible for the "long, dependent human childhoods, so necessary for learning and socialization."

This should come as no surprise to anyone who's ever been properly grandmothered. It may have slipped our minds, briefly, in the haste and chaos of modern life. It has unquestionably been obscured by the fact that in many families today the grandmother is *not* the most senior woman, because her own mother, who may still perceive her as a child, is still living. But we have always known this profound truth, so critically important to all humankind, in our heart of hearts. It is now time for us to remember it, to clarify it, and to celebrate it.

🦋 Getting It All Done Without Turning Your Golden Years into Scrap Metal

The key to grandmothering joyfully rather than fretfully (or worse) has been stated over and over again in this book and is inherent in all of the Grandmother Principles. We can sum it up now as two simple steps:

....
STEP 1. GET ORGANIZED.
STEP 2. RELAX.
....

Nothing in this world is so simple that you cannot, if you really put your mind to it, make it complicated. Because you have so much experience and knowledge, you are superbly equipped to be an expert at making everything burdensome. You have lived so long and been through so much, your mental list of Things That Might Go Wrong is extremely long and detailed. You have more time to devote to worrying than the younger members of your family do, and considerably more skill. You could easily wake up every morning thinking, "Good grief! I know

"Oh, Willard, I never would have guessed the golden years could be such a honk."

eighty-seven awful things that might very well happen before noon today!" after which your only rational course would be to pull the covers up over your head and go back to the merciful oblivion of sleep. Be a wise grandmother: firmly suppress any and all tendencies of this kind.

Most of the time, people who set out for somewhere in their cars arrive safely. Most of the time, people who leave for work in the morning return home safely at night. Most of the time, adults who go somewhere with kids don't come home without them, and they bring them home in good condition. Most of the time, dear grandmothers, people aren't mugged, aren't murdered, don't go bankrupt, don't suffer crippling injuries, don't go to prison, and don't lose their minds. It's true that everyone, including everyone you love, will die—and that's a very good thing, because each generation must make room for the genera-

tions that follow. But most people don't die until it's appropriate for
them to do so.

Our mass media would lead you to believe that it's the other way
around—that the vast majority of us live lives of constant white-knuckled
terror and tragedy and despair. Don't fall for that line. There are people
who live like that, yes, especially in our inner cities, and my heart aches
for them; however, the description doesn't fit most of us.

News is, by definition, what's unusual and different; that's what
makes it news. That's why the media tell us (in revolting and gory detail)
about the one person whose car ran off the bridge into the river on a
given day, instead of reporting on the thirteen thousand six hundred and
eleven people who drove their cars across the same bridge uneventfully
and went on about their business. That's why tiny rural newspapers will
run a headline blaring "Crime rate doubles in county!" after a year in
which four crimes were committed instead of the usual two.

Perverse creatures that we are, we wouldn't turn on our TV sets to
learn about all those boring people to whom nothing terrible has happened. And so the media provide us with what we appear to want:
an unhealthy diet of ghastly stories interrupted only by sports scores,
stock market reports, and commercials. That policy and practice may
succeed in convincing the young and the inexperienced that a typical
life is one perpetually overwhelmed by disasters and gore; it should not
work on grandmothers.

You can drive yourself crazy worrying about all the bad things that might happen to you and to your kids and grandkids. You can drive *them* crazy with your predictions of doom and your checking every half hour to be sure they're all right. You must not do that; it will make your old age a misery.

Your mind can't tell the difference between a real lemon that you bite into out there in the real world and a phantom lemon that you only *imagine* biting into. Real lemon or phantom, when you smell that sharp lemon smell, feel your teeth break through that bright yellow peel, feel that sour juice burst onto your tongue and run down your throat, your cheeks will hurt and your saliva will flow. In both cases, your mind will send out the same message—"Look out! That's a raw lemon you're biting into! That's sour!"—and your body will react in the same way.

The exact same thing holds true when you imagine horrors. Your mind sends out the same "Now hear this! Prepare for catastrophe!" message that it sends when awful things really do happen. This is the core of truth that lies at the heart of much nonsense about positive thinking. Rehearsing imaginary troubles in your mind really does make you a more skilled sufferer. It really does subject your body and mind to stress and strain for which no earthly reason exists.

Every family, no matter what its circumstances, will meet with some misfortunes. You can't keep that from happening. *Accept that.* Do the best you can to prevent troubles, especially the ridiculous kind that can easily be avoided by paying attention and using common sense. Do your best to provide a safe haven when troubles come along in spite of your efforts. Get organized, using the information in this book and your own abundant reliable wisdom. And then—*relax*.

🐾 Coming Up Next

This is the first generation of grandmothers for whom it will be a *common* thing to have their own mothers not only still alive but still active and aware. Everything we know today suggests that

this situation will continue, and that there will be ever more *great-*grandmothers from now on. You are quite likely to live to be eighty, ninety, even one hundred (and more) years old. You will be part of the first generation of grandmothers who live to see their own daughters become grandmothers.

We don't know what this means. We don't know what the set of Great-grandmother Principles might be like. What does it mean for a family to have grandmothers who still have their own mothers to turn to and rebel against? What does it mean for the great-grandmothers, when they find themselves turned to and rebelled against? We haven't a clue! But there are two conclusions that strike me as obvious and unavoidable.

First, the role of grandmother has gained an additional component—that of being safe haven to at least *three* generations, one of which is entitled to criticize the way that's being done. Only a grandmother could manage anything that tricky!

Second, in a very short time we're going to need a book about the role of the great-grandmother, a book that we have never, so far as we know, needed before. I did half a dozen intensive Internet searches, hunting for even one useful resource for the woman who has just learned that she is about to become a great-grandmother. I could not find a single thing! If you know of such an item, please do send me information on where it can be found, because I expect to need it, and I'd like to have it well ahead of time.

I don't know enough about great-grandmothering to write such a book myself. The situation is too new, and there are few role models. I think it's much too simplistic to assume that a grandmother and great-grandmother could function just as "junior" and "senior" grandmothers. Great-grandmothers undoubtedly are going to fill a space in family life that we haven't yet realized is there. Whatever that turns out to be like, I know that grandmothering—provided you know what you're doing— is a joy rather than a burden, and I'm positive that great-grandmothering is also a source of joy—*provided you know what you're doing*. We just have to figure out how it's done.

Someone among you grandmothers out there, someone reading these words this very minute, may well be the person who sits down one day and writes a book titled *The Great-grandmother Principles*. If you don't do it yourself, one of your daughters surely will. If I live long enough, I'm looking forward to reading that book.

◻

Teaching the Grannycrafts

🦋 Thinking Like a Grandmother

Nongrandmothers, as I've said before, tend to be deeply worried about making their mark in the world, about getting ahead, and about "winning." They worry about their "image." Often this means that if they aren't sure they can be an expert at something—fast—they'd rather not risk trying it at all. Grandmothers have the good fortune to be able to set such worries as these aside and concentrate on doing rather than on winning, which makes them superior teachers. The relevant grandmother principle (along with "The grandmother way is the easy way" and "It will be finished when it's finished") is:

••

GRANDMOTHER PRINCIPLE 21:
FOR GRANDMOTHERS, THE LIGHT DOESN'T
HAVE TO BE PERFECT.

••

When I meet people who know I write books, the first thing I hear from at least half of them is that they would write books, too, but they just can't find the time. I resist the temptation to tell them that there are twenty-four hours in their day just as in mine; they already know that.

I hold my peace because I know what their statement usually means. It doesn't mean they don't understand how to parcel out time. It doesn't mean they don't have energy and discipline enough to write books. It just reflects a very common misconception.

Not only for writing, but for every other art and craft and discipline, many people have allowed themselves to be convinced that no work can be done until their surroundings meet a set of Perfection Constraints. Painting or photography can't begin, for example, until the light is absolutely perfect. Poetry or fiction or biography can't begin until a specific kind of pencil has been found and sharpened to a specific kind of perfect point. *Nothing* creative can begin until at least one uninterrupted hour—complete with silence—is available for it. People have heard that great creative minds insist on such constraints and can't create without them; this may be true, for all I know. But although that makes a great excuse, it doesn't apply to the rest of us.

Grandmothers know that creativity is your human birthright and that you go ahead with whatever you have on hand, using whatever bits and scraps of tools and materials—and time—have come your way. Working around those limits is often how interesting new things are discovered and learned, and it has produced many a magnificent patch-work quilt. It's important for you to set an example for your grandchildren that demonstrates this, so that they won't grow up to be the sort of people who are afraid to try anything new and who make lame excuses for never accomplishing anything.

In this section I'm going to show you how to teach one of the basic grannycrafts: how to crochet. Don't be concerned if you are a knitter or whittler rather than a crocheter. That doesn't matter. What matters is that you understand the teaching *method*, so that you can use it to teach your own favorite grannycrafts. Taking a long and careful look at the example that follows will make that teaching method clear to you.

Furthermore, if you've always wanted to crochet yourself, here's your chance to get started. Pretend you're teaching your "inner child." And then, once you have the hang of it, you can teach your grandchildren.

As is true for any written-down set of instructions, you should read these all the way through once, quickly, just to get a feel for what happens, and then go back and begin in earnest.

🦋 Grannycraft Teaching Instructions

🦋 How to Crochet

The first hurdle to overcome, for crocheting, is the idea that boys mustn't learn how. We willingly accept the idea that both boys and girls learn the guitar, for instance, but many people feel that crocheting is for females only. If your grandson's parents feel that way, you'll have to respect their feelings and abide by their wishes. If only the *boy* feels that way, however, you can try to change his mind. Explain that many of the world's greatest tailors and chefs are men who sew and cook (also "girl stuff") extremely well and who have sense enough not to let silly ideas stand in their way. Explain that until very recently sailors on long voyages considered knitting and crocheting and fancy knots to be part of their sailoring, whatever their gender. If that doesn't work, don't waste your time trying to force a change.

"Grandmère—will you please get it straight? It's not like my fiancé, George, HAS a famous chef. It's like my fiancé, George, IS a famous chef."

The second hurdle is the fact that the written instructions are almost impossible to understand, and those with pictures are no less confusing. I taught myself to crochet from written instructions when I was ten years old. For my first project I decided to make bed socks for a beloved aunt (not a wise choice!), and I had to crochet *eleven separate socks* before I managed to make two that were enough alike to be a pair. Today's instructions are not one bit better than those I struggled with so many years ago. It's not that those who write the instructions can't be bothered to do it right; it's just that translating a task that relies entirely on muscle tensions and hand movements into words alone is horrendously difficult. If you can already crochet, you'll be right there to spare your grandchild the misery I went through as I learned; you'll be able to do hands-on showing and helping. If you plan to teach yourself how to crochet and then pass along the skill, what's critical is that you follow the instructions as you read, carrying out each one *while* you're reading. That way, it will all make sense to you. Now, assuming that the child is a *willing* boy (or girl), proceed as follows:

1. Use worsted-weight acrylic yarn—the kind you see in grocery stores and drugstores, the most common and least expensive kind, in a color chosen by the child—and an F hook. Many people try to learn to crochet with tiny little hooks and thread as fine as silk, and they quickly give up in despair; it's like starting the guitar with the hardest chords. F hooks and worsted will do nicely for learning, and won't create artificial problems.

2. The best way to teach crocheting or any other craft is to follow a three-step procedure. First, show the child how it's done; demonstrate. Second, do the task *with* the child, either at the same time (using a different hook) or by holding the child's hands and walking him through the process. Third, have him do it alone. And never hurry him; let him find his own pace.

3. Now comes the step at which beginners tend to get stuck forever: that complicated warble in the printed directions for making the very first stitch. Ignore it! I have been crocheting for forty-nine years and I can't do that yet, but I could crochet a Volkswagen if I had enough yarn. It's not important. Just show the child how to make a loop in the yarn and pull it tight, as if you were making a loop to hang something on a nail. Then tell the child, "Hold the hook in your right hand, between your thumb and your index finger, with the rest of your fingers curled around it. That's right! And take the yarn in your left hand. There you go!" Note: If the child is left-handed, do everything the other way around.

4. Begin by teaching the child how to make a chain. Say, "Hold the knot in your yarn between your thumb and your middle and ring fingers, and wrap your index finger around the yarn coming from

the loop, to hang onto it. That's it! Now put your hook through the loop in the yarn, and *under* the yarn outside the loop. Turn the hook over so that the little jog in it gets hold of the yarn, and pull that bit of yarn right through the loop. That's right—you're getting it! And that's called *chaining*."

Say, "Do that again as many times as you like, until your chain is as long as you want it to be. And as you go, keep moving your thumb and fingers up the yarn *so that your hand feels the same way as it did when you started out and were holding the knot, at the beginning—same place, same position*."

Say, "When your chain is as long as you want it, cut the yarn a couple of inches past the end and pull the cut end through the last loop, all the way, so the hook comes loose. Pull it tight, and your chain is done!"

Now time needs to pass. Most children will have a wonderful time crocheting miles and miles of chains, and you should encourage that. It's usually a mistake to move on to the second step in a process before the first one is understood and under modest control. Let the chaining go on until the child is ready to learn more, whether that takes five minutes or five weeks. Schools have to meet schedules, and they have to get children ready to take tests on specific dates; youth groups such as the Girl Scouts and Boy Scouts and 4H are under pressure to keep youngsters moving along through the ranks, racking up points and badges. Grandmothers, thank goodness, don't have to bother with such artificial barriers.

5. When the child is ready to go on, teach him to do single crochet. Have him chain 5 (do a chain stitch five times) to get started. Then say, "Put your hook through the first chain, the one next to the loop that the hook is in, under the top of the chain. Go behind the yarn you're holding with your index finger, catch it with your hook, and pull it through the chain. Notice—now you have *two* loops on your hook, side by side. Okay? Ready? Go under the yarn the same way

Sewing Doll Clothes

The nuisance part of sewing doll clothes is dealing with the unfinished edges of all those tiny sleeves and necks. The grandmother way is to make sure there *are* no such edges, which is easily accomplished if you use lightweight fabrics. Here's what you do, using a doll's blouse as an example.

1. Cut out two of each pattern piece and lay each pair of pieces together with wrong sides out; use pins if necessary.
2. Sew the pairs of pieces together all the way around, leaving an inch unsewn for turning; trim the edges as close to your stitches as you can.
3. Turn the pieces right side out, finish the unsewn inch you left for turning, and sew the blouse together in the usual way. You're done. (To make a dress you just add a skirt.)

Don't let nongrandmothers tell you this is wasteful because it uses more cloth. The time you save will more than cover the cost of the extra fabric. I made clothes for my daughters this way, by hand, when they were very small and I had no sewing machine. It was magic.

you do when you're making a chain, get the yarn with your hook and pull it through *both* loops. That's right—way to go! Now you have just one loop on your hook—and your first single-crochet stitch is finished."

Have the child repeat this step in the other three chain stitches he has left. And then you say, "That's the end of your first row, and it's time to turn around and go the other way. Pull the trailing yarn through the loop on your hook—just like you do when you start a chain—and turn your work around. Right! Now just do what you did on the first row, and keep going back and forth till the piece is

Making Elegant Outfits in Odd Moments

Choose a sewing pattern that you like, something with simple lines. Cut out the pattern pieces from cardboard or scrap fabric. Crochet the pieces in sport or worsted-weight yarn, *without the seam allowance.* When all the pieces are finished, sew them together. Finish by crocheting around any edges—a good choice is one row of single crochet followed by one row of slip stitch. (This doesn't work well with knitted pieces, unfortunately; knitting doesn't hold its shape well enough.)

as big as you want it to be. And you finish it off the same way you finish off a chain."

You should let some more time pass, until the child feels comfortable with this process. Then he's ready to learn how to follow a pattern and make a recognizable object more complicated than a chain.

6. Have the child use this pattern, which makes nice gifts for parents and relatives and friends:

▶️ BOOKMARK PATTERN
1. Chain 23.
2. Single crochet in 22 stitches, chain 1, turn.
3. Work four more rows the same way.
4. End off.

Show the child how the bookmark pattern would look in a crochet book, so that he can look for other patterns if he likes. It would look something like this:

1. Chain 23; sc in 22 sts, ch 1, turn.
2. Work even for 4 rows; end off.

Traditional Play Dough Recipe

Mix 3 cups of flour, 1½ cups salt, and 6 teaspoons cream of tartar in a big saucepan or Dutch oven. Add 3 cups of water and 3 tablespoons vegetable oil. (If you want colored dough, stir food coloring into the water before adding it.) Mix well, and cook over low heat, stirring constantly, until it begins to form a ball and no longer feels sticky. Turn it out on a board and knead it like bread dough until the consistency suits you. Store it in an airtight container—in the refrigerator is best.

Instant Toys

❖ Cut shapes of any kind that will appeal to the child—dolls, animals, cars, boats, buildings, trees, whatever—from pieces of felt; cut two of each shape. Sew together around the outside edge, leaving a small opening. Stuff lightly with fiberfill, coffee grounds, old nylon stockings, dryer lint, or any other comparable substance, then stitch the opening shut.

❖ Give the child some sheets of paper and a sack of old greeting cards (all grandmothers should start saving greeting cards, from day one), plus tape and/or glue. Add a pair of scissors if the child is old enough to use them safely; otherwise, explain that tearing is not only allowed but encouraged.

❖ Give the child a pair of scissors, glue and/or tape, some sheets of paper, and a stack of mail-order catalogs. Stand back.

❖ For babies, heaven can be found in a batch of food storage containers, especially if they're a lot of different sizes—so they'll stack and nest—and some have lids. You can pick these up for almost nothing at flea markets and yard sales. Give them to the baby in a brown paper grocery bag. Babies love those bags because they make wonderful crackling noises. And they aren't dangerous the way plastic bags are.

7. Now come the explanations, as follows:
   a. "There are lots more crochet stitches you can learn, and there's a way to crochet around in circles instead of back and forth in rows. When you want me to show you these things, just let me know."
   b. "Until you're *very* good at crocheting, you'll want to count the number of stitches you do in every row. It's the only way to be sure that what you're making doesn't keep getting bigger or littler— or both."
   c. "Making a scarf is just like making a bookmark; you just start with a longer chain and go on for more rows."
   d. "You can also make stripes, you know; you just start different rows with different colors."

And that's enough crocheting to lay the foundation.

🦋 General Points

The most important thing for grandmothers to remember, whether you teach the kids guitar or crocheting or piano or tennis or any other body of knowledge, is not to fall into the Law-Enforcement Teaching Style. That is, don't force the child, don't interrogate, and don't spy. Don't say you'll teach her if she promises to practice every single day or twenty minutes a week or whatever. Don't criticize and nitpick and say things like, "Surely you can do better than *that!*" or "Are you *sure* you're really trying?" Don't be forever asking, "Did you practice your guitar today? Do you remember that new chord [or stitch] I showed you?" And don't check up on children by asking the chadults whether they're practicing, how they're progressing, and the like. Everyone else your grandchild learns from may very well teach that way and may feel that no other choice is open to them. You don't have to.

Another useful thing to know is that different children learn better in different ways. The most common difference is a "learning style" breakdown according to the *senses*. Some children learn best when they have something to look at, some learn best by listening, and still others do best as "hands-on" learners. (So far as we know, no children learn best from the senses of smell and taste.)

For the eye kids, let them watch you do things as many times as they like, and always be ready to provide pictures and charts. These kids may learn their crochet stitches more easily if they have pictures to look at.

Ear kids most need to hear you talk, and they may do better if you tape your teaching sessions with them, so they can listen to them again whenever they want. Children who depend heavily on the sense of touch for learning will be helped most when you take their hands in yours and go through the steps of a craft *with* them.

If you're trying to teach a grandchild and nothing seems to work, if the child seems to be struggling without getting anywhere, consider the possibility that you may unknowingly be focusing on the wrong sensory system. Try catering to the other senses and see what happens. If you're not sure which sense your grandchild prefers (or if you're teaching several children at once, and they don't all prefer the same one), be sure you cover all the sensory bases. Teach to the eyes, the ears, and the fingers, all three.

Few things you can do as a grandmother will be more valuable to a grandchild than this sort of teaching. You're not just teaching a craft. You're teaching the child that learning is tremendous *fun*, even if his or her school has classrooms with so many kids packed in for every teacher that learning experiences there are dismal, or worse. You're teaching the child that kids are entirely capable of doing things that are useful and beautiful. You're teaching the child that conditions and materials don't have to be "perfect" before creativity can start. You're teaching the child that everything people need doesn't have to be bought at a store—lots of things can easily be made from scratch. And you're teaching the child, by example, how to teach. These are five important lessons that will stand the test of time and will pay off, over and over again, for a lifetime.

❧ If You're a "Long-Distance" Grandmother

One of the hard parts of grandmothering at a distance is that you can't teach your grandchildren in this way. You can make tapes or videos, of course. I made a "Ukulele Play and Sing Along Tape" for two of my grandchildren, and they were pleased to have it and put it to good use. But it's not the same as being together with the child to provide immediate feedback and praise and help. Perhaps, by the time we have the *Great-grandmother Principles* book that we're sure to need before long, we'll have computer conferencing technology that will make something close to "being there" possible!

References and Suggested Reading

❧ Books

Bernstein, Daryl. *Better Than a Lemonade Stand: Small Business Ideas for Kids*. Hillsboro, Oreg.: Beyond Words Publishing, 1992.
This is a book about businesses for youngsters, written by a young man who was himself a successful youngster-entrepreneur and knows everything there is to know about getting beyond the lemonade stand.

Bodnar, Janet. *Kiplinger's Money-Smart Kids*. Washington, D.C.: Kiplinger Washington Editors, 1993.
For adults as well as children, this book offers the clearest explanations of financial and business terms and concepts that I've ever seen, and is packed with resources for the otherwise neglected realm where grandmother/grandchild economic issues overlap. I wish I'd had a copy of it available when I was still a woman totally ignorant of finance and business; it would have saved me from making many foolish mistakes.

Brookes, Mona. *Drawing with Children: A Creative Teaching and Learning Method That Works for Adults, Too*. New York: Jeremy P. Tarcher/ St. Martin's, 1986.
I couldn't draw at all until I tried this book (and it wasn't because I'd never tried any of the others that claim to teach drawing). This really

works and is filled with creative ideas that grandmothers and grand-children can collaborate on. It teaches you a sort of "drawing alphabet" —a set of basic shapes and figures, all very easy to do, that both you and your grandchildren can combine into drawings that will amaze you. For the "long-distance" grandmother, it's also a book for learning how to illustrate letters and stories and cards for your grandkids with your *own* drawings.

Carlson, Charles B. *Buying Stocks Without a Broker.* New York: McGraw-Hill, 1992.

Dacyczyn, Amy. *The Tightwad Gazette: Promoting Thrift as a Viable Alternative Lifestyle.* New York: Villard Books/Random House, 1992.
This is an excellent source of ideas for almost-free presents and games and "stuff" for grandchildren—plus much useful information for grand-mothers (even those who don't care to reuse their vacuum cleaner bags).

Drew, Bonnie, and Noel Drew. *Fast Cash for Kids: 101 Money-Making Projects for Young Entrepreneurs.* Hawthorne, N.J.: Career Press, 1995.

Elgin, Suzette Haden. *The Gentle Art of Communicating with Kids.* New York: John Wiley & Sons, 1996.
This book will explain to you both why good communication across the generation gap is so critically important today and how it can be achieved. It's based on contemporary linguistics and my *Gentle Art of Verbal Self-Defense* system, tailored specifically for language inter-actions between youngsters and adults.

———. *"You Can't Say That to Me!": Stopping the Pain of Verbal Abuse— An 8-Step Program.* New York: John Wiley & Sons, 1995.
When people ask me, "If I can only have one *Gentle Art of Verbal Self-Defense* book, which one should I get?", this is the one I recommend. It presents the basic *Gentle Art* system, with scenarios showing it in use between parents and kids, spouses, parents and chadults, in-laws, doctors and patients, teachers and students, employers and employees, and more. There are lots of dialogs, plus workout sections for practicing your skills.

Faber, Adele, and Elaine Mazlish. *How to Talk So Kids Will Listen and Listen So Kids Will Talk.* New York: Avon Books, 1980.

This classic book on communicating across the generation gap has wonderful comic strips and vast amounts of really good information. I recommend it highly.

Kitzinger, Sheila. *Becoming a Grandmother: A Life Transition.* New York: Scribner/Simon & Schuster, 1996.

In this book, Kitzinger does some very unusual things. She has researched the grandmother role all over the world, and the book provides a broader view of grandmothering than you can get from grandparent books written only for the United States and Canada. The research is solid and thorough, but the book doesn't read like an anthropology text. It's clear and nontechnical and informative.

Kornhaber, Arthur, Sondra Forsyth, and Betty A. Prashker. *Grandparent Power: How to Strengthen the Vital Connection among Grandparents, Parents, and Children.* New York: Crown Publishing, 1995.

Not just for grandmothers, this book by the "Dr. Spock of grandparenting" and his coauthors is packed full of helpful information for both grandparents.

Mariotti, Steve. *The Young Entrepreneur's Guide to Starting and Running a Business.* New York: Times Books/Random House, 1996.

Everything you could possibly need to know in order to help your grandchildren start their businesses and succeed with them: how to write a business plan, how to keep accounts, what to do about taxes, how to handle cash flow, how to choose a business, and much more. Combine this book with Bernstein's *Better Than a Lemonade Stand,* Bodnar's *Kiplinger's Money-Smart Kids,* and the Drews' *Fast Cash for Kids* (all cited above), and you'll have a complete basic business and finance library for your grandchildren (and you yourself) to learn from.

Wasserman, Selma. *The Long Distance Grandmother: How to Stay Close to Distant Grandchildren.* Point Roberts, Wash.: Hartley & Marks, 1996.

Wasserman devotes hundreds of pages to telling you exactly how to grandmother at a distance, covering in great detail many topics I've only had room to touch on briefly. She devotes a lot of space to step-by-step instructions—easy to understand and follow—for making books for your grandchildren yourself. Highly recommended.

🦋 Articles

Begley, Sharon. "Your Child's Brain." *Newsweek*, February 19, 1996, pp. 55-61.
This (with the article by J. Madeleine Nash listed below) will explain why the things that grandmothers can do with grandchildren are so crucially important—to the grandchildren and to all of humankind.

Callahan, Sidney. "The Grandma Hypothesis: Wallpaper She Ain't." *Commonweal*, August 15, 1997, pp. 7-8.

Goodman, Susan. "Arthur Kornhaber: A Few Grandparenting Lessons from America's Most Outspoken Grandpa." *Modern Maturity*, January–February 1997, pp. 53-56, 68-71.

Jones, Tony. "God and Scientist Reconciled." *New Scientist*, August 10, 1996, p. 46.

Maynard, Fredelle, "To Mother, in Loving Memory." *Woman's Day*, May 16, 1995, pp. 79-80.
Maynard, Joyce. "I Remember Mom." *Woman's Day*, May 16, 1995, pp. 77-78.
Here we have something unique to the Sandwich Generation! Both of these pieces are tributes to the writer's mother, and they cover three generations; Fredelle Maynard is Joyce Maynard's mother.

Nash, J. Madeleine. "Fertile Minds: Special Report." *Time*, pp. 47-56. (See also the article by Sharon Begley, cited above.)

Sheehy, Gail. "Congratulations, You're a Grandmother." *Oakland Tribune*, August 14, 1996.

Index

A

Abilene Paradox, 100
active life style, value of, for health, 147
advice, grandmothers', 28–29, 44–45,
    62–63
    unsolicited, 74–75
    See also storytelling and family myths
aging, with grace, 152–57
apathy (medical), in children, as health
    warning, 140
appearance
    of grandmothers, 9, 10, 25, 26
    of ill grandmothers, 148–49
    of old women, 152–53
arguments, family, 72–79
authoritarianism, in grandmothers,
    42–44
autobiography, as type of family
    history, 180

B

baby-sitting, 45–46
barter banks. See family barter bank
behavior, grandchildren's, grand-
    mothers' rights to change, 51–52
Bernstein, Daryl, Better Than a Lemon-
    ade Stand: Small Business Ideas for
    Kids, 115
blame, grandmothers' taking, 80–82
bloating, 143
Bodnar, Janet, Kiplinger's Money-Smart
    Kids, 92
books
    for adults, on grandparenting, 49, 67,
        115, 116, 120, 207–10
    for grandchildren, 164
"boomerang kids," 114
bribing, 57
bumps on head, 140
burial, expenses of, 120

business, teaching grandchildren how
to manage, 112–17

C

cakes, icing, 87
calendars, to deal with family
gatherings, 100–101
cards, sending, 68
Carlson, Charles B., *Buying Stocks
Without A Broker*, 120
cassette tapes, 65, 148, 167
for family history, 179–80, 184
for long-distance teaching, 206
chadults. *See* children, grandmothers'
own
charms (medical), 143–45
childproofing, 98–99
children
learning styles of, 204–5
See also children, grandmothers' own;
grandchildren
children, grandmothers' own (the
"chadults")
benefits of grandmothers to, 20
after death or divorce of one, dealing
fairly with the survivor, 127–30
grandmothers' taking responsibility
for behavior of, 134–35
greedy, 117–18
perceptions of grandmothers by,
vs. grandchildren's perceptions of
grandmothers, 41
Children's Book Committee, 164

Chinaberry Catalogue, 164
coherence, grandmothers' maintaining
of, 29–31
comfort given by grandmothers, 28–29
to losers, 75–76
communication
with frightened grandchildren,
52–56
with grandchildren who are
underdogs, 59–60
hostile and negative, avoiding, 50
with negativity-expressing
grandchildren, 62–63
pitfalls of, 50
with unwilling grandchildren, 57–59
See also storytelling and family
myths
computers, 47
for creating family history, 179
See also Internet
confidants, grandmothers as, 73–79,
162–63
confidences, always kept by
grandmothers, 74
consistency, grandmothers'
maintaining of, 29–31, 89–90
conversation
teaching grandchildren the rules of,
54–56
See also communication
cookies, piecrust, 87
copy machines, 38
crackers, toasted, 87
crafts, teaching to grandchildren,
195–206

criminal acts, of grandchildren, 134

crises, 127–29

    grandmothers' taking charge of parenting in, 81–89

    incorporating into family histories, 133–36

    multiple, triage in, 130–32

    stages of, 128–29

crocheting, teaching to grandchildren, 197–204

D

dangers, worrying about, 188–89

DayTimers, gift of, to grandchildren, to help them get organized, 114

death

    financial preparation for, 119–21

    talking to children about one's own, 150–51

decision-making, grandmothers' role in, 79–81

diaries, as gifts, 69

diarrhea, 143

disability insurance, 106

discipline, secondhand, 44

disgrace, 134–36

divorce, of grandparents' own children, effect of on grandchildren, 127

doctors, "bothering," in emergencies, 141

doll clothes, sewing, 201

D.R.I.P. (direct re-investment) stocks, investing in, 120

E

eccentric grandmothers, 17–18

e-mail, 47, 48–49

emergencies, 122–36

    real vs. phony, 123–27

    regarding health issues, 137–38

emotional work

    grandmothers' role in accomplishing, 67–72, 85–89

    of men vs. women, 70–72

employment, teaching grandchildren fundamentals of achieving, 113–17

encouragement, grandmothers' giving of, 53, 56

energy, grandmothers' recognizing limits of own, 96–105

engagement calendars, as gift, 69

estate planning, 119

euphony, in family stories, 164–67

F

families

    grandmothers' benefits to coherence of, 22

    histories of. *See* family history

    large, keeping track of everyone, 39

    writing assignments for, 183

family barter bank, 109–11, 114, 131, 132

family disagreements, grandmothers' role in mediating, 72–79

family gatherings, 69, 100–102

family histories, 68, 167, 173–87
   assimilating crises and emergencies
      into, 133–36
   reasons for, 175–77
   technicalities of creating, 177–84
   time taken to make, 173–75
   turning over documents to family
      members, 184–87
family loan fund, 106–9, 114
family newsletter, 31–40, 46, 167, 183
fear, grandmothers' role in coping with,
      in grandchildren, 31–40, 46, 52–56
fever, 140
financial experts, in estate planning, 119
follow through, 58
Foundation for Grandparenting, 93
funerals, expenses of, 120

G

gardening, 94, 147, 155
gender equity/inequity
   in business and money matters, 116–17
   in crafts, 197
   in kinship tasks, 69–72
gifts, 37, 68, 69, 114
   buying in advance, 148, 149
   no strings attached, 185
grandchildren
   benefits of grandmothers to, 21
   books for, 164
   changing the behavior of,
      grandmothers' rights in, 51–52
   multiple, 104

perceptions of grandmothers by, vs.
   grandmothers' own children's
   perceptions of, 41
teaching crafts and practical skills to,
   195–206
grandfathers, 23
grandmothering
   benefits of, 20–23
   choosing not to do, 19–20
   from position of illness and
      infirmity, 146–51
   value of, to grandmothers, 22–23
   See also principles of grandmothering
grandmothers
   attitude toward media doom news,
      189–92
   basic skills of, 11–12
   bedridden, 151–52
   benefits from, to the family, 20–23
   children's vs. grandchildren's
      perceptions of, 41
   as confidants, 73–79, 162–63
   image of, maintaining, 89–90
   importance of, 187–89
   long-distance. See long-distance
      grandmothering
   longevity of, 187–89
   shortage of competent, 10–12
   stereotypes of, 9–10, 50
   types of, four basic, 14–19
grandparents, resources for, 93
Grandparents' Day, 191
great-grandmothers, increase in,
   193–94
greed, in families, 117–18

grief, 134
guilt, 64, 134–36

H

headaches, 140–41
health, 137–57
    basic information on, in children,
        139–42
    emergencies, 137–38
    See also illness
health insurance, 106
Hedging, 78
helping, of family members,
        appropriateness of, 105–11
helplessness, vs. wellness, 147
homemaking skills
    crafts, 195–206
    gifts, 69
    recipes, 87, 156, 203
    toys, 203
honesty, in grandmothering, 45–46, 83,
        159–61
hostility, in language, 77–79
house-cleaning, 84, 85–88
humor, in crises, 133

I

icing of cakes, 87
illness
    causes of, 137
    common childhood illnesses, 141–42

    grandmothering from position of,
        146–51
    See also health
image, grandmothers' maintaining of,
        89–90
information, sharing of, solicited and
        unsolicited, 44–45
injuries, 139
insomnia, 143
insurance policies, 105–6, 119–20
Internet
    health resources on, 141
    investing sites for children on, 116
    resources for grandparenting on, 93
    support group sites on, 83
investing
    for grandchildren, 92–95, 116
    teaching grandchildren about, 114–15,
        116
itching, 143

K

kinship, maintaining within a family,
        67–72
Kitzinger, Sheila, *Becoming a
        Grandmother*, 6, 67
Kornhaber, Arthur, 22

L

large families, 39
learning styles, of children, 204–5

lecturing, need to avoid, 44–45
letters, 48–49, 65
   unanswered, 64
lies, in name of larger truths, 158–61
life insurance, 105–6
listening, 54, 55, 57, 74
loans, family fund for, 106–9, 114
long-distance grandmothering, 46–49,
   65
   and creating family histories, 187
   in crises and emergencies, 136
   emotional work of, 91
   and teaching, 206
losers, grandmothers' comforting of,
   75–76
loss of face, 77, 79
love, grandmothers' assurance of, 53,
   56, 61, 76, 135
lunches, ideas for, 156

M

Mariotti, Steve, *The Young Entrepreneur's Guide to Starting and
   Running a Business*, 116
martyrs, grandmothers assuming role
   of, 45–46, 83, 91
mediating, grandmothers' role in, 68,
   72–79
medicines, grandmothers' principles
   on, 142–46
memorabilia, 182–84
memory, deterioration in, 71
men, and emotional work, 70–72

metaphors, power of, in
   communicating with children,
   54
Miles, Susan, 83
money
   assisting family members with,
      appropriateness of, 105–11
   availability of, in crises, 127
   explaining management of, to
      grandchildren, 111–17
   managing, for grandchildren,
      92–95
multiple crises, triage in, 130–32
multiple grandchildren, 104
myths, family, 159–61. *See also* story
   telling and family myths

N

National Foster Parent Association,
   83
nausea, 143
negative feelings of grandmothers
   about certain family members,
   avoiding expression of, 63–65
negative messages, how to
   communicate, without causing
   someone to lose face, 76–79
negative questions, avoiding, 59–60
newsletter, family, 31–40, 46, 167, 183
news stories, grandmothers' attitudes
   toward, 189–92
notebooks, as gifts from grandmothers,
   37

O

office supplies, 33, 177
organization, 189
overburdened grandmothers, 18–19

P

pain, 137–38, 143
panic, and health issues, 138–42
parenting, grandmother assuming role
    of, in crises, 81–89
parents, grandmothers' own, 130
perfectionism, 186–87, 195–97
personal taste, vs. being a positive role
    model, 63–65
pets, 147
photographs, family, 68, 181–82
play dough, recipe, 203
political correctness, 66
potions, 145–46
precedents, setting carefully, 103–5
prescriptions, grandmothers', 143
pride, 52, 60
principles of grandmothering
    list of, 24
    1. The grandmother way is the easy
       way, 27
    2. Grandmothers already *have*
       tenure, 27–28
    3. Everything comes to an end
       eventually, 28–29
    4. A grandmother is a safe haven,
       29–31

    5. There's nothing so simple that
       you cannot make it complicated
       if you really try, 38–39
    6. The most powerful way to teach
       is by example, 41–44
    7. People with *real* clout don't *have*
       to throw their weight around,
       44–45
    8. Grandmothers don't *have* to be
       politically correct, 66
    9. When getting somebody else to
       do a task is more work than just
       doing it yourself, do it yourself,
       66–67
    10. Most arguments are about who is
       in charge, 73
    11. It's always *safe* to talk to a
       grandmother, 73–75
    12. Grandmothers *delegate*, 88–89
    13. A grandmother is not a
       quarterback, 97–105
    14. *Somebody* has to be the grown-up,
       123
    15. No sickness or injury is so bad
       that panic can't make it a lot
       worse, 138
    16. There are secret stories that only
       grandmothers should know,
       162–63
    17. It will be finished when it's
       finished, 173–75
    18. Grandmothers plan for the long
       haul, 176–77
    19. If it can't be done one way, it can
       be done some other way, 180

principles of grandmothering *(cont'd)*
20. After you give people something, it belongs to *them*, 185
21. For grandmothers, the light doesn't have to be perfect, 195
privacy, 74, 162–63
property, dividing up among heirs, 120–21

Q

questions, negative, avoiding, 59–60
Quill Office Products, 33, 177
quitting, 60–62

R

recipes
easy, 87, 156
play dough, 203
relaxation, 189
reliability, grandmothers' maintaining of, 89–90, 95–96
resources for grandparents
articles, 210
books, 207–10
Internet sites, 93
responsibility, grandparents' taking of, for behavior of adult children, 134–35
role models, grandmothers as, 40–46
in communication, 63
and greed, 118

positive, vs. personal quirks of negativity, 63–65

S

Sandwich generation, 131
secrets, 74, 162–63
self-control, in grandmothering, 43–44
sewing, 201
shame, 52, 54, 134–36
Sheehy, Gail, 10
sickness. *See* health; illness
society, benefits of grandmothers to, 23
Spock, Dr. Benjamin, 140
stability, grandmothers' maintaining of, 29–31, 127–28
stepchildren, dealing fairly with, 129–30
step-parents, 129–30
stock investments, 120
stomachaches, 140–41
storytelling and family myths, 54–55, 62–63
collecting and managing, 163–67
creating them, 167–72
reasons for, 161–63
See also advice, grandmothers'; myths
strength, grandmothers' maintaining, in crises, 127–28
support networks
on Internet, 83
in multiple crises, 131, 132

T

taking charge, 81–89

tangible property, dividing up among heirs, 120–21

teaching methodologies for grandmothers, 40–44

  things to teach grandchildren, 113–17, 195–206

telephoning, 47–48, 56

therapists, 163

time, grandmothers' recognizing limits of own, 96–105

toys, handmade, 203

traditional grandmothers, 15–16

travel, with children, tips for, 96

triage, in multiple emergencies, 130–32

truths, vs. small lies, 159–61

U

ultramodern grandmothers, 17

uniforms, grandmothers', 26

V

ventilating, expressing negative feelings, 118

W

wakes, 133–34

Wasserman, Selma, *The Long Distance Grandmother: How to Stay Close to Distant Grandchildren*, 49

wealth, recognizing and dealing with, 119

WebTV Network, 49

wellness, vs. helplessness, 147

wills, 119

winners, in arguments, 76

worry, about danger in modern world, 189–92

Z

zipper songs, 166

❦ CARTOON CREDITS

❦ Chadults' Birthdays

_____

_____

_____

_____

_____

_____

_____

_____

_____

_____

_____

_____

_____

_____

🦋 Grandchildren's Birthdays

_____

_____

_____

_____

_____

_____

_____

_____

_____

_____

_____

_____

_____

❧ Special Family Occasions

🦋 About the Author

Suzette Haden Elgin, author of the best-selling *Gentle Art of Verbal Self-Defense* series and a grandmother of ten, has a Ph.D. in linguistics from the University of California San Diego, and is a novelist, poet, and artist as well. Founder and director of the Ozark Center for Language Studies, which she operates from her home in Arkansas, she is nationally recognized for her seminars and public speaking.